Peeking Over the Edge

... views from life's middle

Also by Cathy Marley

Breathing Again ... thoughts on life after loss

Love in Bloom
with *Women Writers of the Desert*

Peeking Over the Edge
... views from life's middle

Cathy Marley

Copyright © 2006 by Cathy Jo Marley

All rights reserved. No part of this book shall be reproduced or transmitted in any form or by any means, electronic, mechanical, magnetic, photographic including photocopying, recording or by any information storage and retrieval system, without prior written permission of the publisher or author. No patent liability is assumed with respect to the use of the information contained herein. Although every precaution has been taken in the preparation of this book, the publisher and author assume no responsibility for errors or omissions. Neither is any liability assumed for damages resulting from the use of the information contained herein.

Reviewers may quote passages for use in periodicals, newspapers, or broadcasts provided credit is given to Peeking over the Edge by Cathy Marley. Contact: Cathy Marley at CJM@CathyMarley.com.

This is a work of non-fiction and names have been used with permission.

ISBN 978-0-9990518-3-2

Cover photography by Cathy Marley

Back Cover photography by Lena Anita Tamboli

Published by:

CJM Press

CJM Press,
Phoenix, AZ
www.CathyMarley.com
Email CJM@CathyMarley.com

Printed in the United States of America

Printed on Recycled Paper

Published March 2006
Second edition April 2018

ॐ

For Norm,
who gave me wings
and the courage to leap off the cliff
and SOAR.

Grateful acknowledgement is made for permission to reprint excerpts from the following copyrighted works:

BOTH SIDES NOW
Words and Music by JONI MITCHELL
© 1967 (Renewed) SIQUOMB PUBLISHING CORP.
Copyright Assigned to CRAZY CROW MUSIC
Used by Permission of ALFRED PUBLISHING CO., INC.
All Rights Reserved

THE ROSE
By AMANDA MCBROOM
© 1977 WARNER-TAMERLANE PUBLISHING CORP.
and THIRD STORY MUSIC INC.
All Rights Administered by WARNER-TAMERLAND
PUBLISHING CORP
Used by Permission (pending) of
ALFRED PUBLISHING CO., INC.
All Rights Reserved

THE GREAT MANDELLA (WHEEL OF LIFE)
Words and Music by PETER YARROW,
ALBERT GROSSMAN and MARY TRAVERS
© 1967 (Renewed) SILVER DAWN MUSIC
All Rights Administered by WB MUSIC CORP.
Lyrics Reprinted by Permission (pending) of
ALFRED PUBLISHING CO., INC.
All Rights Reserved

OKLAHOMA CITY TIMES
Words and Music by PAUL HAMPTON
(c) 1968 (Renewed) WB MUSIC CORP.
Lyrics Reprinted by Permission (pending) of
ALFRED PUBLISHING CO., INC.
All Rights Reserved

Acknowledgments

This book was a long time coming – sixty years, in fact. You see, it took me that long to discover my passion. And, it took more than time. It took relentless self-exploration on my part, but most importantly, it took endless encouragement on the part of a great many very special people. They have my deepest gratitude.

My most profound thanks go to Norm, my kind and patient husband of thirty-two years. Your unconditional love and very public pride in every word I write has inspired me to keep trying whenever I doubt myself. You are the foundation of my world. And whenever I write of love, I am inspired by thoughts of you and David, Dale and Dennie, the incredible human beings I am honored to call "my" children.

To the Dream Builders sisters of my heart, Anita, editor extraordinaire, and Elaine, I can only say this book would never have reached the light of day without your reassurances that what I have to say matters. You listened to every word, praising the effort if it was good, gently guiding if it was not. If Norm is the book's father, you are its midwives.

Special thanks go to the Women Writers of the Desert, especially Linda Holter Arellano, Margie Beus, Lisa Hall Bomar, Vivia Giovannini, Marilyn Haight, Betts McCalla and LinDee Rochelle. I am in awe of the talent residing in you all. Being one of you inspired me to believe I could make the giant leap from "writer" to "author."

And my deepest gratitude goes to the extraordinary women of Entrepreneurial Mothers Association for the first little newsletter column that grew up to become a book. Your tears and laughter taught me that my words do have the power to touch hearts. Thanks to EMA must include its founder and my dear friend Kathy Stephens who simply sat down one day and wrote a book, all the while claiming she didn't know how to write. You, Kathy, made me believe I could do it too.

Thank you, too, to all the precious friends who begged me to keep writing so they could read **more**. You know who you are. And finally, I must thank my tremendous clients at CJM Communications who trusted this simple wordsmith to put their brilliance into words. You helped me ease into this author thing by letting me write your words first.

Thank you, one and all.

Cathy Marley

*"This little light of mine
I'm going to let it shine
Oh, this little light of mine
I'm going to let it shine
Hallelujah
This little light of mine
I'm going to let it shine
Let it shine, let it shine, let it shine"*

**This Little Light of Mine
Composer Unknown**

Contents

Acknowledgments i
Preface 1

Chapter 1: Sags & Wrinkles & Ups & Downs…this little body of mine 3
   In the Mirror 5
   Diets 9
   Transformation 13
   Marks of Time 17
   The Doll with the High Heels 21

Chapter 2: Looking In, Looking Out…this little self of mine 25
   Hero Worship 27
   A Perfect Life 33
   Mush Brain 37
   A Story of Two Ovaries and a Womb Unused 41
   A Lighter Load 45
   The Right Age 49
   The Elephant in the House 53
   Keeping the Pack Light 57
   Natural Talents 61
   A Singing Heart, a Dancing Soul 65

Chapter 3: Joys & Magic & Bright Red Hearts…this little love of mine 69
   The Little Rose Bush That Could 71
   On Love and Valentines 75
   New Faces, Exotic Places 77

Someday Is Today 81
Mothers and Daughters 85
Rich Girl, Poor Girl and Simple Abundance 89
Bungee 93
The Christmas Angel 95
Grow Up! 97
Magical Fifty 99
Heroes, Heroines and Bodice Rippers 103

Chapter 4: You & Me Together...this little world of mine ***107***
I Believe in One World 109
Winged People in Feather Coats 113
Smile! 117
First Day, Last Day 119

Chapter 5: Today, Tomorrow & For Always...this little legacy of mine ***121***
Peeking Over the Edge 123
Ah Spring! 127
The White Suit 129
Things Change 133
Paths to the Future 135
Pea Salad 139
Gossamer Threads 145
Just a Stepmother 149
Esther's Shoes 153
Remember Me 157
Ripples in a Pond 159

What Is Real? ***163***

Eagle's Home ***165***

About the Author ***169***

Preface

It happens all too often when we reach middle age. One day we wake up, we look in the mirror and realize we are fifty. Suddenly, we come face to face with our own mortality. Well, sometime between forty-five and fifty, I woke up and smelled that particular pot of coffee. I looked at my life and found contentment and security and love. I saw a family and friends that made life worth living. I had work that was at once rewarding and challenging, but a single burning question colored it all. "What mark," I wondered, "have I made on the hearts of others?"

I needed to know the world would be a better place for my having lived and that when I am gone I will be remembered as more than just a woman who put in her time. I would like to believe I will be remembered for my positive outlook and my desire to find the good in any situation I encounter. That desire especially applies to all the negatives we hear every day about growing older. Being over 50, I believe, is not the end of life's joys and adventures. It is, rather, the beginning of the best life has to offer. We grow wiser, calmer, and far more loving as the flower that is our life reaches its fullest bloom.

I want to be known as a woman who lived her passion. Without passion, I know my legacy would be faint indeed. In her seminal book, *Inventing the Rest of*

Our Lives, Suzanne Braun Levine says, "When ignited, whether it is a pilot light or a blinding light, a passion illuminates the inner recesses of who we are."

This book is the love-child of a creative passion for the beauty of words that re-ignited in me as I approached my pivotal fiftieth birthday. It is a celebration of the wisdom the years can give us. It is my way of shining a positive light on whatever life may bring. In it you will find me, heart displayed for all to see. I hope you will also find yourself. If you do, please let me know. I welcome your story at www.CathyMarley.com.

Chapter 1

Sags & Wrinkles & Ups & Downs ... this little body of mine

*"But I see your true colors shining through
I see your true colors
That's why I love you"*

True Colors ~ lyrics by Thomas Kelly
& William Steinberg

"There comes a time in life when finally (how long has it taken?) you are simply true to yourself. Like breathing, you instinctively follow your truest impulse for that has led you well for years and you trust inside and it shows in the beauty that you, finally, own."
                              Vanity Fair Advertisement

☙

In the Mirror

Somewhere along the way to middle age, I stopped looking at myself. I suppose as this face and body became predictable to me, I simply didn't feel the need to look at them too closely. Waking up in the morning, I rarely needed the mirror to tell if they were having a good day or bad. I just knew by how I felt. For years, clothes and grooming received cursory attention at best. Buying new clothes, something I dearly love, came down to a simple matter of whether something was too tight, too short, or the wrong color. Most days, a quick glance in the mirror, a fluff of the hair, lipstick, eyebrow pencil and refreshed blusher meant I was ready to go. But take a close look at the whole image? Not a chance! You see if you only focus on your head when you look in a mirror, you don't really have to see the wrinkles or the sagging rear.

Well, today I really looked at my body. For once, I actually saw everything below the neck. I took a long hard look at it, flaws and all. It was the first time I've done that in a very long time and believe me, it was traumatic.

The mirror caught me at a weak moment. It was one of those times I was actually doing something very good for myself. I was exercising. I was at a Pilates studio and like a carnival funhouse, there were mirrors everywhere! Trainers tell you that the mirrors are there so you can monitor your form, but I think it's to keep you aware of how you really look. Catch a glimpse of all that bulging flesh in Spandex and it's impossible to ignore yourself.

Well, that's what happened to me. Even though I've been avoiding mirrors for a long time, today I could ignore them no longer. There I found myself, sitting what I thought was straight and tall on a Pilates Reformer, proud to even be doing such a rigorous workout. And then I saw myself. All I could think was, "Oh…My…God!"

My trainer Brenda has been working with me for almost three years. We started when I actually discovered exercise for the first time in my life - sometime around the age of 54. I thank Brenda for helping me start. Without her pushing me to get my butt moving, I would have surely continued aging far more rapidly and with much less grace. Before I began working out with her as my trainer, I had started to feel the stiffness and slow motion that herald decline in no uncertain terms. After three years of workouts, though, I was feeling pretty good about myself. My flexibility had returned and I was proudly sporting muscles!

But today, as I perched on the Reformer and worked to attain proper form and breathing, the mirror was right there! I couldn't avoid it. And what did I see? I saw a rear end that actually hung over the edges of the platform. The biceps I had grown so proud of had mysteriously sprouted wings below their strong bulge! My legs, strong though they were, gave new meaning to the term "thunder thighs!" And, based on my aching abdominal muscles after every session, I knew I had abs hiding somewhere under that flabby belly, but I couldn't see them for the fat.

Where, I wondered looking at the reflection, was the woman I kept seeing inside my head? I kept looking for that strong, taut figure but somehow, she kept hiding behind that sweaty middle-aged woman on the Reformer. Beyond all rationality, my mind hoped to see the image transformed by some magic trick, maybe with a little smoke to go with the mirrors. A big part of me wanted to see the strong, young, straight me of thirty who still lives inside my head and my heart. That was the me who was concentrating so fiercely on becoming fit. Instead, what I saw was the reality of a fifty-seven-year-old body that has been allowed to have one too many of its beloved Krispy Kreme doughnuts and nowhere near enough vegetables and physical activity.

Now, I have never had any pretensions at a model-perfect body. And by and large, I've learned to accept that petite is not something I will ever experience. But, I've also learned that mirrors never tell the entire story. They only show the outer shell. Most of the time, that's enough. Today what I saw in the mirror was reality. It blindsided me. I could not restrain my shock at what I saw, and my reaction leapt its way unbidden to my lips. I think the words "fat" and "ugly" were prominent in what I said.

Brenda's loyal response was immediate and deeply sincere. "You could never be ugly," she reassured me with a powerful hug. "You are far too beautiful inside. What's outside doesn't matter at all." It brought tears to my eyes as it opened them to a profoundly moving truth. I realized that the way I look is nowhere near as important as the way I am.

I was reminded of an interview with Celine Dion I had seen on television. As she almost negligently indicated her lovely, unlined face, she said, "Growing older, everything goes down, but your spirit goes up." That is the woman Brenda helped me see today.

I know as a young woman my face and my body were still defying gravity as they can only do in the young. But my youthful body was paired with the heaviness of spirit, the angst that comes to the young who worry about the world and the future. Now, as I am in my middle years, the face and body I saw in the mirror today can no longer defy gravity. Nor should they try. But I also know that my spirit has cut the bonds of worry. Freed of gravity, it soars! That is the spirit that can look into the mirror and, seeing a fat gray-haired old lady, peer beyond the reflected image to see and accept the generous, loving heart beating within.

"What some call health, if purchased by perpetual anxiety about diet, isn't much better than tedious disease."
George Dennison Prentice

Diets

In my lifetime, I have tried almost every diet known to man. I have tried low calorie, low carbohydrate, low fat, low just about everything out there. I have tried Weight Watchers (twice), Jenny Craig, Atkins, Overeaters Anonymous (also twice!) and Nutri System. I have even tried Slim Fast, grapefruit, shots, and, when they were still prescribed by some doctors, amphetamines (never again!!!).

I started dieting somewhere around the age of twelve when my mother first took me to a doctor for my weight. She knew how unhappy I felt about being overweight and tried valiantly to make sure I moved into adolescence in something approaching a normal sized body. But somehow, every attempt eventually failed. Afterwards, I always managed to find every single pound I had lost, plus some I didn't know were lost. I guess they missed me and brought their friends when they returned.

With each failure, I became a little more suspicious of the promises made by the next diet to come along. Still, I tried one after another, ever hopeful

I would find the magical quick fix for everything that was "wrong" with me. I don't know for sure when it happened, but one day I woke up and decided I was through with all the "diets." I made the decision to simply eat sensibly and accept my body as it was, a major leap for a woman who had always fought the self-esteem battles that come with extra pounds.

That was also about the time I finally started to exercise for the first time in my life. I think the two happened when they did because I finally recognized that the important thing was not the shape I showed, but the shape I was in. I finally understood health was the most important thing and looks secondary. With fitness came a more robust health and a somewhat improved shape. I decided I could happily live with such a good balance.

In my mind, spending my entire life worrying about every bite leaches pleasure from life! Not too long ago, I observed a group of people at a buffet dinner in a friend's home. One person said, "Oh I can't eat anything white." Another said, "No carbohydrates for me!" Yet another was avoiding fat while others shunned meat. As I took measured portions of everything, I found myself thinking, "Every one of these people is obsessed with what they cannot have! Their whole lives revolve around what they can and cannot eat! And it has been that way for years with marginal results." Then I realized that I have friends I am rarely able to share a meal with because they are always on one diet or another. I miss them. Through all my years of one plan after another, I have learned that constant dieting is no way to live fully.

Peeking Over the Edge

Today, I have reached a point in my life where I know that the body I have is mine. I own it. For as long as it remains healthy, I accept it, good or bad, fat or thin, for the healthy gift it has been for so many years. I have learned that some of us are destined to be unbearably thin. Others, like me, are challenged every day by the love of good food and a metabolism that does not always accommodate it. Is there another diet in my future? Probably. I think I will always want to live in a more normal body, but if I ever do diet again, it will be for keeps. Until that day comes, though, I will accept what I have.

I look in the mirror and know I inherited my Aunt Thelma's body. For years I focused on that single connection to my aunt, seeing only the body resemblances. What I missed was the warm heart and generous nature that unselfconsciously lay within that ample body of hers. It is only in recent years that I see and accept the greater inheritance I received from her and treasure the warm spirit she passed on to me.

For now, I choose to focus on what I can have and the abundance of gifts that have come my way in this lifetime. There is a certain sense of freedom that comes with that. My world becomes one of abundance with food in its rightful place in the Universe. It ceases being the center of my existence and becomes something enjoyable that just happens to keep me alive. I think that's where it belongs.

"Getting my lifelong weight struggle under control has come from a process of treating myself as well as I treat others in every way."

Oprah Winfrey
O Magazine, August 2004

Transformation

In recent weeks, hand in hand with a significant weight reduction, I have been surprised to discover a wee streak of vanity in myself. I am primping far more often than ever before. I pause at mirrors, captivated by an image I don't always recognize. Sometimes I find myself actually turning to take a quick look at a backside that no longer seems to be mine. I have started adding color to my hair to cover the gray. And for the first time, I am indulging in regular pedicures, manicures and facials.

At 58, this newfound vanity is something of a surprise since I have never thought of myself as a particularly vain woman. After all, anyone who goes through life carrying more than just a few extra pounds rarely has that luxury. I suppose a small part of me always envied women who had legitimate grounds for vanity. After all, they had the advantage of self-confidence and a fair share of natural beauty.

Despite my size, I have usually paid attention to my appearance, making the effort to do my hair, wear a little makeup, and dress well (even though real fashion stopped at size fourteen for many years). I think it may have been my way of compensating for a less-than-ideal body. Perhaps it helped mask the overwhelming lack of self-esteem that I felt for so much of my life.

You see, no matter how hard I tried to make it untrue, much of my self-image was irretrievably linked to my size. I suppose that's the curse of many seriously heavy people. For years, I irrationally believed if I could only lose weight, everything else would magically fall into place for me. I would learn to love myself. Everyone else would love me unconditionally. My children would be perfect. My husband would be uncharacteristically adoring and romantic. I would be wildly successful at whatever I chose to do, and I would learn to love exercise! Is it any wonder that my diet efforts always failed? How could any one action ever do all that?

Somewhere in my thirties I began to change. I reversed the order of my expectations. First, with the excuse that they never worked anyway, I quit dieting. Then I began working, seriously working on getting my heart straight with myself. I attended a series of multi-day seminars and through the insights I gained in those long days, I finally began learning how to love "me." The concept of "love thyself first, everything else will follow" finally started to sink in and become real in my heart.

The changes were gradual at first. Most, something like an earthquake that happens in Alaska and causes tidal waves thousands of miles away in Hawaii, were taking place far below the surface, but their effects were far-reaching and profound. I don't think I was even fully aware of the incredible shift that was taking place in how I was relating to the world around me, but the changes were happening, and I was growing.

I became more positive. Gradually, I began to stop worrying about what others thought of me. I discovered that most people didn't actually think of my failings nearly as often as I did. Nor did they think of <u>me</u> as much I thought they did. Then, several years into the process, I lost the job that had defined my identity. I would have thought I'd be devastated. After all, I had built much of my life around being in a technically and intellectually demanding position at a large corporation. But I was far from devastated. I was, in fact, elated.

Suddenly, I had the freedom to choose whatever I wanted to be. I had a husband who loved me enough to give me that liberty, to support me while I found my true calling. It was an incredibly freeing experience. And in time I did find that calling. I began to write. I discovered a voice I had never known was hiding within the depths of my heart.

One small step at a time, that self-realization brought with it the happiness and fulfillment I had always expected to be a result of my diets. As I learned to love myself, my children, my husband, everyone began to seem more loving in my eyes. I earned a respect for my professional abilities that far outstripped anything I had known before. It was an exhilarating experience and it took me years to become accustomed to it, to have it slip around me like a warm, comforting cloak.

After that, the exercise part of my transformation was easy. I was ready for it when I did a little work for an exceptional personal trainer and she offered to get me started. For the next three years, I focused on building the strength that seemed to have abandoned me as I aged. And build it I did, growing stronger every day. But my old nemesis – fat – was still lurking in the shadows.

One day it just seemed as though everything came together at once. I realized that I was happy. I was fit. Only one thing was missing. I wanted the body I had never been able to achieve. I found myself finally ready for the diet I had always thought must come first. In the real world, it had to come last.

For once, the regimen of a restricted diet felt natural. The pounds began to fall behind me. They landed alongside my old negative thoughts and joined hands with the sedentary "me" who didn't understand how to love herself. A new me emerged like a butterfly from a cocoon. With the transformation came a small streak of what many would call vanity. But I give it another name. Unlike vanity that touches only the surface, this reaches to the very core of my soul. I call it pride. That is the true transformation.

"Wherever you are, whatever your circumstances may be, whatever misfortune you may have suffered, the music of your life has not gone. It's inside you -- if you listen to it, you can play it."
                                    Nido Qubein

☙

Marks of Time

For Christmas one year, I gave my granddaughters Aimee and Ilyse their very first makeovers. It was my way of helping them step gently into an adult world they had been eyeing for many years. I think learning skin care and how to apply makeup with a subtle hand is a major rite of passage for a girl. It is somewhat equivalent to a boy's first real shave. I have heard that boys see that shave as a step into their father's adult shoes. Likewise, a young girl's first touch of pink lipstick and mascara is a symbolic leap into the full bloom of womanhood.

It seemed appropriate for these two twelve-year-old girls to discover their new skills at the side of older, wiser women, women who understand the deeper significance of that first touch of feminine wile. And so, I invited their Aunt Dennie, my daughter, and Ilyse's mother Kay to join us as we learned the mysteries of Mary Kay from my friend Robin. My great room was filled with the sparkle of feminine laughter that day as we gathered - three generations of women - all passing different mileposts along life's highway.

As young teens, my granddaughters were poised at the beginning of what is arguably life's greatest adventure - adulthood. With their porcelain skin, clear eyes, and taut bodies, they hummed with youthful vitality. Life had yet to mark them with the deft, artistic hand that etches character into our faces as we age. I would rather they never have to face any of life's more difficult paths, but I know they will. I can only hope that with the resilience of youth and caring, loving guidance, they will hurdle their obstacles with heads held high and eyes fixed intently on the future's brilliant possibilities.

Looking around the table, I could see the first marks of time and life in the other two faces. My daughter and daughter-in-law teased one another unmercifully as they noted eye crinkles and laugh lines that we all knew would someday morph into full-blown wrinkles. But in these two women, a graceful maturity had emerged. I could see shadows of both sorrow and joy lurking in their eyes and defining the lines they carry with pride. Life has thrown some of its larger challenges at them - one widowed at 34 with an adolescent son to raise, the other in the midst of a life-changing divorce. Looking past their stressed postures and rather worried faces, I could see resilience in these two, but there was also strength and character - confidence that regardless of the challenge, they have the power to prevail.

As for me, looking in the mirror that day revealed a different reality. Oh sure, I saw the lines, sags, and graying hair that come with more than 50

Peeking Over the Edge

years. But I knew a secret they all had yet to learn. I knew that beneath the aging skin that no longer seems to fit quite right beat the heart of youth, tempered with life's wisdom. I looked into my own reflection and peeking back at me was the dewy teen I had once been and the strong woman I have become and all the women I have been between the two.

As Robin so beautifully put it to us that day, "Women don't age. They only become more interesting." Well, I would like to believe that as I continue to nurture myself on life's juices, I will grow and become more interesting with every day. Perhaps growing through all the years of our lives is what keeps us truly young. Although I can't *know* what will be happening in my next moment, in any of my tomorrows, I can still use each day to fill myself with the ever-changing fascination and excitement of life - never aging, only growing more interesting!

You can domesticate your body, but you can't domesticate your face – even by having a lift or having your nose bobbed. A face bears the reflection of our nature, which in the beginning is veiled by the attractiveness of youth. But as soon as youth begins to go, everything written on the face starts to come to the surface, and pretty soon it's engraved there. No landscape can equal a human face that's been molded by its own character."

Francoise Giroud
With Bernard-Henri Levy in
Women and Men (Little, Brown)

☙

The Doll with the High Heels

Her name was Cissy. To my little girl eyes, she was the most exquisite thing I had ever seen, tall and brunette, with a perfectly formed woman's body — complete with slender waist and perfectly proportioned breasts. She was clad in entrancing, crisp white organza, the long, full skirt trimmed in tiny red roses and lace, the entire outfit complemented perfectly by bright red high heeled sandals. She was grace, beauty, poise — womanhood at its best.

It was love at first sight that summer of my tenth year. Day after day, I would return, merely to adore her beauty in wide-eyed wonder and dream of the day I too could be as perfect. Always, she would calmly gaze back at me from her lofty position, just out of reach, on a high shelf in our neighborhood toy store.

As Christmas neared, my obsession grew. I begged my parents, Santa (I still had a marginal vestige of belief), anyone who would listen. One gift and one gift only could make me happy — the doll with the high heels. By Christmas Eve, I was sobbing in my father's arms, convinced Santa would never bring her for me. After all, she was much "too expensive." You see, we were far from wealthy and in 1955, $20 was an exorbitant sum for a mere doll. Still, on Christmas morning, there she was under the tree, a luminous testament to the truth of Santa Claus and the love of two parents who made a child's dream come true. It was a magical Christmas, lightly slipping treasures of memory into my waiting heart, storing them away to later remind me of forgotten love, dreams come true, and the simple joys of childhood.

After that Christmas, new dolls never again seemed so important. Oh, I probably received them for the next two years or so, but for the life of me, the only doll I remember to this day is Cissy. For me, she was the realization of an impossible dream. Even now, she remains my most conscious evidence that my parents truly loved me and that the magic of Christmas can never die.

Always before, my dolls had been baby dolls or little girls with flat feet, straight bodies and innocent looks. Cissy was different. She was a woman. Discovering her, I first began glimpsing brief flashes of my own future adolescence and adulthood. Cissy represented an unreachable ideal, but I was blind to its impossibility. I believed I could grow up to be just as lovely, just as perfect as she. Even though I lost track of her along the way, her perfection was somehow always the mirror I held for myself in my deepest heart as I grew into womanhood.

Then, one day well into my own middle age, I found Cissy again. With little thought for what she had meant to me, I had casually stored her away in a box in a storeroom on our farm. After years in that dusty room with its tiny, sharp-toothed predators, she was a very sorry sight indeed. Bald and naked, with fingers chewed away, a large crack in her head, and lashes long gone from her lovely blue eyes, she was still recognizable to my heart.

Heartbroken at the ravages I had allowed, I wrapped her broken figure in a soft towel and carried her to a nearby doll hospital where we found a wig to cover her baldness and broken head. It wasn't quite the sassy, dark brown style she had worn in her newness, but somehow its new upswept look was fitting for her restoration in middle age. Finding a picture of her original dress, I had it duplicated. It too was different, not quite as crisp and young-girl fresh as the original, but I think it was fitting as well. Some things — the fingers and eyelashes — could never be repaired. They stand today as a testament to the challenges she has faced in this life. And even though I searched everywhere, I was never able to replace her shiny red shoes. But it doesn't seem such a great loss that she is barefoot in her later years. Perhaps shiny red high heels are best relegated to the young anyway.

I believe the new Cissy has far more character than the original. In her youth, she was an almost-impossible ideal. Today, she wears her life proudly, missing fingers and all, content in what she has become — as am I. We may no longer be the epitome of grace and youthful beauty, but we are still womanhood at its best, serene in a life lived fully and content with the marks it has left upon our bodies and our souls. With that, who needs red high heels?

Chapter 2

Looking In, Looking Out ... this little self of mine

*"I've looked at life from both sides now
From win and lose and still somehow
It's life's illusions I recall
I really don't know life at all
I've looked at life from both sides now
From up and down, and still somehow
It's life's illusions I recall
I really don't know life at all"*

Both Sides Now ~ lyrics by Joni Mitchell

"Whoever you are there is some younger person who thinks you are perfect. There is some work that will never get done, unless you do it. There is someone who would miss you if you were gone. And there is a place that you alone can fill."
                                                Jacob M. Braude

Hero Worship

When I was growing up in Texas, my sister was my hero. I adored her. With eight years between us, she was already in high school and dating when I began first grade. I wanted to do and be everything she was. From my child's perspective, she stood ten feet tall and could do absolutely nothing wrong.

Oh, I'm sure that as little sisters go, I was very much the pest. I remember my parents insisting that she and her date sometimes take me to the drive-in movies with them. I can imagine her reaction, but she took me anyway. Then, as soon as we arrived, she would send me to play at the playground conveniently located just below the giant screen and comfortably far from the car. For a teenager on a date, it was a very smart move because I would happily stay there playing until the final credits rolled!

Eventually, being along on those dates made me think I could be a part of other dates as well. One evening I decided to invite myself to go with them. As an 8-year old, I thought it was a marvelous idea to hide in the back seat of her boyfriend's car, just to see what they did all those times when they went out without me. Imagine my surprise when all they did was park the car on a nice quiet side street just a short drive from our small-town home. Curious, I waited to see what would happen next. Well, they got very close together. I waited some more. Then I figured it out. They were kissing and that was all they were going to do! Unable to control myself, I popped up and with a delighted laugh, exclaimed, "Surprise!" Needless to say, the evening ended very early.

Looking back, I'm not sure I understand why my sister put up with all my silly pranks, but she did. Sometimes, she even volunteered to take me with her. One of my fondest memories is just the two of us sharing root beer floats at the local A & W drive-in. I don't remember what we talked about, but we would sit in the car, drinking our root beer, eating ice cream, and finding some common ground despite the age difference. Every time she did something to include me, my sister grew even taller in my eyes.

As time went on, I developed my own friends and interests. Gradually, I just stopped following my sister around. I'm sure she was very grateful, but knowing life as I have experienced it now, I'm also sure that some part of her missed our connection. Eventually, she went away to college, career, and marriage, moving farther and farther away with each step in her life. But always, she remained firmly perched high on the pedestal I had built for her when I was a child.

She was the role model that shaped many of my choices through high school and into college. I studied math and German, not because of any special interest or aptitude, but because my beloved sister had studied both. I dreamed of sororities, and proms, and dormitory life —— all part of her experience. But for me those things were not meant to be. My life was meant to take a different path.

In time, our lives naturally began to diverge. Eventually I realized I would never be everything she was. A small part of me was disappointed with myself even though if I had examined my heart, I would have known trying to imitate her was burying my own individuality. Gradually, though, I did let go and I began moving along my own path, not one I had modeled after my sister's. I suppose that was when my own light began to shine.

Still, my sister remained my hero and as hero and acolyte, there was always something of a distance between us. For years, she remained the adult to my child. Then through a series of events, that changed. One day, battling dysfunctional demons she had always so successfully hidden from me, she let go of her role as protector and came to me for support, much as I had come to her so many times. Always, she had rescued me. Now it was my turn. Over the thin, tenuous lines of the telephone, our hearts reached out to one another and we forged a new, stronger bond based on our love for one another as equals.

Cathy Marley

When I look back on our relationship, I remember the early days with sweet nostalgia, but it is the more recent years, the years since my sister's pedestal toppled, that I treasure the most. They are based on our respect for one another. You see, I discovered that hero worship is a very poor substitute for respect. It makes us blind to the other person's failings and burnishes their positive attributes far beyond their natural ability to shine. I believe to have a truly honest connection to another person, we must see their failings as clearly as their strengths and love and respect them anyway.

Respect is what I found when my sister slipped off the pedestal she never really wanted in the first place. Seeing her, finally, on my level, I saw a woman I could respect for her true accomplishments and for having overcome obstacles in her own path. I saw a woman with incredible perseverance and tenacity. They were traits that brought her through lows I could only imagine. I saw a woman whose strength and intelligence somehow managed to pull her through when others would have failed. And I saw a woman whose generosity of spirit began showing very early in life at an A & W Root Beer stand with a little girl who worshiped her.

Do I still feel some hero worship? Of course I do. The true heroes in our lives don't stop being heroes just because their pedestals shrink or are removed entirely. We just see them differently. My sister's pedestal no longer puts her above my reach. It is still there, but now it is on a level that allows me to step up and be her equal as we both become our very best selves. In some ways

Peeking Over the Edge

that makes us both heroes. Holding tight to one another, we can reach for others who are ready to step up and stand beside us as they seek the best in themselves and the world. You see, the pedestal may not be so very tall, but there is lots of room at the top. All of us, heroes in one way or another, have earned the right to stand on a pedestal every now and then.

"Much of the time, going through life is like going through the airport steering a loaded luggage cart with one bad wheel. Sometimes you just feel ridiculous, sometimes you actually look ridiculous, and sometimes all you can do is try to push it in generally the right direction."
Marilyn vos Savant

ଓ

A Perfect Life

There was a time in my growing up years when I knew exactly how my life would unfold. I knew that one day I would fall in love, marry, give birth to beautiful, intelligent children, and live happily ever after. I would have the perfect husband ... always loving, attentive, and sharing all my interests. And I would have the perfect children ... handsome, educated, successful and always immaculately dressed. It would, in short, be the perfect life ... filled with comfort and the many worldly luxuries enjoyed by the characters in the books I read. Oh, I was intelligent enough to know that a vision of total perfection was a fairy tale more than reality, but I still believed my life would be closer to my idea of perfection than not.

Well, of course, as real life would surely have it, one day I did fall in love. Deeply. Hopelessly. Beyond all reason. And, with a man thirteen years my senior.

With him came a ready-made family of two teenage sons and an adolescent daughter.

I had dreamed of passing on my love of art and literature and refinement to children I could mold in my own image. But that was not to be. Rather than molding my own children, I found myself striving to set an example that I could only hope would eventually impress itself on minds already largely shaped. My dreams had seen preppie sons and a ruffles-and-lace daughter. Instead, love brought me rowdy 4-H cowboys and a tomboy more comfortable with horses than with dolls. It was love that kept me there and whispered to my heart, telling me to plant my seeds anyway and be patient while they grew.

As a young woman, I had dreamed that when I was gone, some small spark of ME would be left in this world, perhaps my offbeat sense of humor, my love of books and language, or my acceptance of all points of view and lifestyles. I believed that could only happen by passing my genes to a child of my own and molding that child from birth. I learned that is not necessarily true.

Today, I look at David and Dale, my cowboy sons, and I see two men who have learned to value words. They may not read as voraciously as I, but they do read. And they enjoy it. Sometimes, we talk of ideas and world affairs, discussing our deepest spiritual beliefs or the latest political controversy. When we do, I find their minds fascinating, challenging even, as they follow lines of logic that would never have come to me on my own. They never did become preppies. With the stoic honesty of two John Waynes, they are cowboys at

Peeking Over the Edge

heart yet today, and that is fine with me. It is their essence I appreciate, not the external surface.

And my tomboy daughter Dennie still prefers jeans to dresses. Now, as a woman, she values down-to-earth fairness, inner strength and character far more than prom queen vanity. She can take care of herself, no matter what she wears. She has become a strong, beautiful woman whose intelligence and honesty shine in the male-dominated career she chose. I believe that is so much more important than frilly dresses, dolls or all the plays and symphonies she could ever have seen.

That youthful dream of the perfect life came true after all. It just never formed the way I expected it to. I know now that when I am gone, my memory will carry on in faint echoes of refinement and culture that have quietly slipped into the lives of these remarkable three people and their children and their grandchildren. It lingers in their lives when they pick up a book and think of me or when they see a particularly lovely painting and appreciate its composition and color. It is a legacy well worth leaving behind. It has been the perfect life.

I found a quiet place today in the hustle and bustle of my life. I didn't think to go searching there, and really, I didn't find it, it found me. All this time-- this quiet place I longed for was within me."
                                     Beverly Tribuiana-Montez

Mush Brain

I think I have a terminal case of mush brain lately. You know, it happens on those days when you make your to-do list then, at the end of the day, can't remember whether you did any of it or not. Did I call the people I said I would? What about the faxes? Did I send them? Uh-oh, what did I tell that client I would do? And when?!!! This week I've called people twice, each time for the same reason and on more than one occasion, sent others to the wrong source for the answer to a problem! I think to myself, "What in the world is happening to me? Am I losing my mind? Could it be that old age has finally caught up with me even though I've been running as fast as I can? Ohmigod, maybe I'm in the early stages of senility!"

Well, I don't think so! I think what I really have is a common, but rarely acknowledged, malady. As we try to keep all the balls in the air at once, eventually one bounces off the tips of our fingers and all the rest come tumbling down behind it. I'll bet I'm not alone. I'll bet that what I'm going through this week happens to every one of us at one time or another. Think about it. See if this scenario sounds even vaguely familiar.

You're leaving on vacation in five days. One of them is a holiday, so of course you take that day off to be with your husband, your friends, your family, etc. That leaves four days. Now, you've got an important new client and you <u>must</u> finish her job before you leave - hello late nights! But, you also need to pack, shop, and generally prepare to be gone a week. Add to that a daughter or grandson with a birthday (while you're gone, of course!), a home alarm that keeps going off for no reason (call the alarm company!), and a phone that rings every five minutes (always important, often business), and a best friend who just fell in love and really, really needs to talk. I think you get the picture! Been there, haven't you? Small wonder our brains sometimes turn to mush and we short circuit!

I think God should give each of us our very own personal angel. You know, someone like the tooth fairy - someone to pat us on the head and say, "Here's your lollipop, honey." Of course, that lollipop is not a reward for bravely losing a tooth, but for not losing your mind while you've kept all the balls in the air.

On the other hand, maybe we all already have a personal angel. Maybe it's the client who says, "I love your work! You make me look so good!" Or perhaps it's the child who wraps her arms around your knees, looks up at you in wide-eyed adoration, and says, "I love you mommy. You're the bestest mommy in the whole wide world." It could even be the grandson who says, "Thanks, Gramma, I really needed your help

Peeking Over the Edge

today. You're always there when I need you." Or maybe it's simply the husband who, recognizing the frayed end of your rope, enfolds you in his arms, hugs you gently, and loves you in spite of your mushy, disorganized brain! Maybe those personal angels are all around us after all, pockets full of lollipops, just watching the world's greatest juggling act and waiting to catch us when we slip!

"Most of us miss out on life's big prizes. The Pulitzer. The Nobel. Oscars. Tonys. Emmys. But we're all eligible for life's small pleasures. A pat on the back. A kiss behind the ear. A four-pound bass. A full moon. An empty parking space. A crackling fire. A great meal. A glorious sunset. Hot soup. Cold beer. Don't fret about copping life's grand awards. Enjoy its tiny little delights. There are plenty for all of us."

Untied Technologies Corporation
advertisement

ॐ

A Story of Two Ovaries and a Womb Unused

Tonight, as I wander in reverie among the dreams I discarded as I made my way through life, one dream calls out to me with particular poignancy. It is the dream I held close to my heart from the time I rocked my first baby dolls in my arms - the dream of motherhood. I discarded that particular dream long ago when I made a very adult decision to not give birth to children of my own. I know it was the right choice for me, yet it is still a dream that calls to me as it lies abandoned beside the path I walk tonight.

Cathy Marley

I find myself, unable to sleep, musing on that long ago choice. I suppose the sleeplessness comes in part from a choice more recently made and in part from a cold that, like a thick quilt snugged around my head, fills it with stuffiness and pads my brain. Both are important to this story.

In talking with others about my decision to have a hysterectomy, I have put up a brave front, making light of the whole idea of ending my child-bearing years with the decisiveness of a slamming door. But in my deepest core I know there is some sadness at the finality of it all. Again, I know the decision is right. After all, I have been in full menopause for a very long time and birthing children is no longer an option. I suppose that slow dwindling of my life-bearing force really marked the letting go of this particular dream. In my head, I left it behind long ago, but without my realizing it, the baby-dream still kept tenuous strings attached to my heart. Admittedly, those strings grew weaker with each passing year, but they were still there. Now I am allowing those strings to finally break. Therein lies the sadness.

Tonight, as I lay sleepless, I came face to face with the fact that in two weeks, I will walk out of a hospital and leave behind parts of my body that for much of my life were ready to give me that dream. Month after month, the sturdy, dependable ovaries sent their tiny eggs drifting along to a womb that would have happily nurtured that child I had decided to forego. They were good organs, rarely giving me trouble. But now, after 57 years, they do. Maybe the small sadness I feel is in abandoning them, unused, to some anonymous and impersonal surgical death.

But here, I come to the story of my cold, for it is the gift of the lives I chose to nurture instead. You see, the kisses and powerful heart hugs of two-year olds are impossible to resist, even knowing that they carry a price of sniffles and stuffed head. Even with that price, they are joy.

I like to believe that these grandchildren of the children I chose to nurture are, here in my later life, the purest manifestation of those mother-dreams lying behind me. They affirm to me that the organs I am choosing to place reverently alongside that long ago dream did not function in vain. Their dependable cycles kept reassuring me that I was the mother I needed to be, the mother I was meant to be. It's only fitting that I leave them, together with the dream, in a place of honor on that gentle slope that is my past.

"I've found with age comes a gentleness, and you have just more appreciation for life and what's important in life, and you think about taking more time to enjoy people."

Pam Del Duca
President & CEO, the Delstar Group

A Lighter Load

I'm a pack rat. In fact, I'm a *serious* pack rat. Sometimes I think I never learned to throw anything away. My closets overflow with enough clothes to stock a small boutique – with multiple sizes, yet! I've collected enough office supplies to keep several offices running for months. And books! I'm sure I could build my own library – complete with reference section. On top of everything else, I collect things! That's just a more structured and acceptable form of being a pack rat, you know.

I think you can see the picture. The fact of the matter is that the longer I live the more "stuff" I seem to collect. Actually, I like most of my stuff. It's comforting. My world is filled with things I enjoy. It's interesting. No, it's crowded! Some days, I look into the future and I have nightmares of stories I've read about old ladies living in houses with narrow paths through their hoarded possessions. All too often, they die in its midst and never see that they've missed an opportunity to experience true freedom.

You see every one of us builds our own hoard of stuff as we move through life. Some is just more obvious. The material pack rats of this world are easy to spot. We're the ones blissfully threading our way through the chaos of our many possessions, hardly seeing that our paths become increasingly narrower.

Hardest to pick out, though, are the emotional pack rats. They hoard feelings, clinging tightly to every experience – the good *and* the bad. As the years go by, they can't understand why they have become so cynical and negative in their outlooks, not recognizing that they have clogged their hearts and souls with collections of negative experiences. Just as the material pack rat clings tenaciously to "things", so too does the emotional pack rat hold tightly to every past hurt and grief. Only in letting go can either achieve a measure of freedom.

I have decided it's time to start clearing out the debris of stuff I've collected over the years. Oh, I'll probably never get rid of it all, but I know that every time I let go of something, I'll feel lighter, less constrained. I've started with my office and am already more productive and far happier to work each day. I think I'll tackle closets next. That's a huge task, but I know I'll feel better with every thing that goes.

You know, as I work through the physical clutter, I'm tossing the emotional dead weight too. For some

Peeking Over the Edge

reason, it surprises me that 58 years of emotional baggage is riding out the door with all the other "junk." It shouldn't, but it does. Already, I can feel something opening inside myself. My heart seems to be expanding to hold the joys of life. Is that freedom I see in my future? I think so!

"Breathe. Let go. And remind yourself that this very moment is the only one you know you have for sure."

Oprah Winfrey,
O Magazine, September 2002

☙

The Right Age

The older I get, the more convinced I am that people are never happy with their age. At seven, I believed ten was a magical age. Something about the double digits made me think that would be a most grown up age to be. But ten came along and I discovered that it was really no big deal. My parents still treated me like a child even though I was sure that magical tenth birthday should have made a significant difference in what they allowed me to do. In my mind, I was ready for freedom, but nothing changed! I still had to live by the rules. Ten was not yet the right age.

Oh well, I thought, maybe things would be different once I was a teenager. And so, I yearned for the swift passage of those three more years. Teen. The very idea was alive with possibility. I was positive that once I reached the "teens," I would surely be grown up and allowed to make my own choices. But then that eagerly anticipated day arrived, and it wasn't quite so special after all.

Cathy Marley

    I had believed my thirteenth birthday would be an event worthy of fireworks and grand announcements of new freedoms, but I turned thirteen a scant five months after we buried my mother. All I wanted for that birthday was to have her back. The freedom I had dreamed of was mine for the taking, but at a bittersweet price. An emotionally bruised and often-absent father and responsibility for a puzzled and lonely younger brother thrust an adult world upon me far sooner than I had believed possible. I learned that thirteen should never be the age a child steps into the adult world. I needed to be a child just a little bit longer. Thirteen was not quite the right age.

    A year later, with my father remarried, I focused instead on twenty-one as the age of true adulthood. My teen years flew by in a haze of parental control made bearable by the thought of impending freedom. By my twenty-first birthday, society said, I would be an adult. But when that day finally came, was I? I think not. Oh yes, I was able to vote and drink and live on my own, but I was still a self-centered and immature child in an adult body. At twenty-one, living the frivolous life of a single, unattached woman, few really took me seriously. Worst of all, I had not yet learned to take myself seriously. Twenty-one was still not quite the right age.

    Somewhere in the fifteen years after my twenty-first birthday, though, I must have missed that right age. With what I saw as the cowled specter of middle age looming before me in my thirties, I began to feel faint twinges of dread rather than anticipation as each new birthday neared. I held tenaciously to a youth I so feared

Peeking Over the Edge

losing - but losing it was inevitable. And still no age was ever quite right.

Many of us focus our middle-aged eyes so intently back at our lost youth that we fail to see every day's precious moments flying by like telephone poles outside a rushing car. Until one day, when we must stop - never having known the *right* age. In focusing only on the past or the future, we discover, we have forgotten to enjoy *now*. We find ourselves at sixty or seventy or even one hundred, still looking for joy or enchantment or fulfillment.

Living in anticipation of tomorrow or regret for yesterday is such a waste of a life. Having done that for far too many years, I have learned regardless of where I am in life, I must cherish each moment as a priceless gift and live life to its fullest. For me, this day, this moment, is the time of my life! I choose to live life's breadth as well as its depth, knowing that finally I am the right age.

"When we truly care for ourselves, it becomes possible to care far more profoundly about other people. The more alert and sensitive we are to our own needs, the more loving and generous we can be toward others."

Eda LeShan

The Elephant in the House

There's an elephant in my house. I think it's probably been living here a long time, but I just noticed it. More likely, I've known it was here all along, but it's been here for so many years I just stopped seeing it. I know I have been walking around it every day. I've decorated it, dusted it, even fed it prodigiously. Still, no matter how much I ignore it, it remains a very large presence in my house, a presence that rarely becomes the topic of conversation. But when it does surface, somehow I always manage to change the subject pretty quickly and divert attention to some smaller, more innocuous creature. You see, I don't find this particular elephant especially attractive and I suppose I would prefer to simply deny its existence.

I finally acknowledged my elephant this year after a visit to my doctor for my annual physical. For several years in a row, he had been diligently pointing out the increasingly skewed numbers that were showing up in my blood chemistry. Once, we even threw medication at the numbers and, temporarily, they became a little more normal, only to fly more out of whack in subsequent years. With each physical, my doctor would point to the elephant and say, "You really need to do something about that. Get rid of the elephant, and all of these problems will go away. Keep the elephant, and you can expect it to eventually run amok. The numbers will only get worse." Until this year, I always agreed with him, then went on my merry way and did nothing about the elephant. After all, it was my elephant and I was comfortable with it even if I never talked about it and ignored its presence.

This year, that changed. I suppose it was a brief series of seemingly unrelated events that opened my eyes and brought me to finally acknowledge my own big grey beast. First, I lost a much-loved mother-in-law. Then my sister told me about her newly-diagnosed diabetes. Next that physical came along and this year the numbers were seriously frightening. All of this was topped with the death of one very precious friend of many years and a health scare from yet another. The effect of one blow after another was cumulative and caused me to begin thinking about my relationships with the people I love - my husband, my children and family, my dearest friends.

I've always known how very much I value these people. They are the bedrock of who I am. Sometimes I find myself reflecting on how very empty my life would be without them. It is these relationships that give my life meaning. Take them away and my direction drifts away as well.

What I never realized was how ego-centric my perspective had become. It was that perspective that allowed me to ignore the elephant for so long. The shift happened when I realized the loved ones I worry about feel the same way about me! I suddenly found myself thinking, "If I worry about losing them, do they not also worry about losing me? I have this huge elephant that is a serious threat to my own health and as long as I choose to ignore it, they love me enough to not confront me with their own concerns. It comes down to one simple fact. None of us is talking about the elephant in the room."

With that one thought, the elephant suddenly became very real and I found myself tripping over it every time I turned around. I could ignore it no longer.

You see, feeling the fear of losing someone I love is one thing. Even though I know losing them would be unbearably painful, I can learn to live with the fear and not let it control my life. But, realizing I am causing the same fear in others is intolerable. I cannot live with that because it would mean consciously hurting those I love. This is why I am finally talking about the elephant, committing myself to removing it from my life even though my plan has dangers that frighten me. After all, elephants, no matter how domesticated, are known to fight when cornered. But go it will. It is the only way I can find to save myself and in doing that, ease the fears of those I love.

I think we all have elephants of one breed or another in our own homes. And it is far easier to see someone else's elephant than it is to see our own. I look at friends and acquaintances and every one has an elephant of some size trailing around close behind them. I question how they can allow those elephants to remain. After all, I ask, don't they care about how it is affecting them? The funny thing is, some of the elephants I see in other homes are so very similar to my own. Why, I wonder, if I can see other people's elephants so clearly, has mine taken so long for me to recognize? Maybe it's simply a matter of perspective. Perhaps it has just taken this long for me to view myself through the hearts of others. I think that may well be the best way to see. It certainly keeps the elephants away.

"Your choices today determine your tomorrow and you make your life through the power of choice."
                                    Kathy Smith

Keeping the Pack Light

Sometimes I think my life has been a little like a long distance race, one that started with me carrying a pack lightly filled with everything I would need for the run. Along the way, I spotted some pretty cool things that I was sure I would need to help me finish the race as a winner. One by one, I picked them up and put them in my pack, each time increasing my load just a little bit more. For a long time, I didn't notice the extra weight.

Some of the things I picked up hatched like mysterious alien eggs into not-so-pleasant monsters with sticky hands and feet. Once I had them, they did not want to go away and clung to me like nasty little slugs. They made my pack noticeably heavier.

Well, I am now well into my sixth decade and I've decided it's time to lighten the pack. Some of the things in there, things like honesty and self-esteem and good relationships, are treasures and worth keeping. They may add a little bit to the load, but they make me a better person and will surely fulfill their original purpose. I think I'll embrace those and hold them close all the way to the end of the race.

Much of what is in my pack is neither treasure nor trash. It's just stuff I picked up because it was pretty, and its sparkle caught my eye at the time. Not really seeing an immediate use for it, I convinced myself that it was worth picking up anyway, just in case. I'm sure I thought I could find a use for each and every thing I added. Some I did – some I did not. I'm pretty sure I no longer have a use for things like pantyhose and high heeled shoes and the chains of vanity that attach to them.

Even so, knowing there are treasures still in the pack, I'm looking closely at this middle ground between trash and treasure. I think it is time for me to sort the gold from the pyrite. I'll keep the gold. It's worth the weight. And I'll pass the rest along to someone who really can use it to run a better race. After all there are women out there who love pantyhose and spike heels, aren't there?

But the ugly little monsters will have to go. I don't need them. In fact, I never did. They just took up space and weighed me down. Sometimes I ask myself why I picked up things like a focus on everything a less-than-ideal adolescence denied me. That little monster smiled prettily at the time and offered a convenient excuse for everything that went wrong in my life. But it wasn't really that pretty when I picked it up and it got uglier as time went on. Once it was fully hatched, it was so ugly and heavy that it slowed me down to a crawl. I know for sure it took up far too much space in my pack of life. I shudder to think of all the joys I missed because they couldn't fit in there next to that victim story. I'm consigning that little beastie to a flaming pyre

Peeking Over the Edge

so it never again has a chance to attach itself to any unsuspecting little girl I know.

The thing is, something about turning fifty started me peeking into that pack. Like a four-year old with bulging pockets, I found things in there that needed to go to make room for even greater treasures. For almost ten years now, I have been sorting through it, poring over one thing and then another. As the pack gets lighter, so do I. The race has stopped being a race. Instead, I sometimes run for the sheer joy of running. Sometimes I stroll. Other times I dance. And sometimes I do pick stuff up because it's pretty. I look at it and then I put it back for someone else to find. That keeps my pack light and makes the rest of my journey so much easier.

"Listen to the passion of your soul, set the wings of your spirit free; and let not a single song go unsung."
                                   Sylvana Rossetti

☙

Natural Talents

Have you ever looked at your face in a 5x magnification mirror? First of all, you must get very close to even focus. And when you do, all you can see are the flaws; huge pores, coarse hairs and minute changes in smoothness that might presage a pimple! It's almost like looking at your own face under a microscope that by its very magnification keeps you from seeing the harmony of the whole. I have done that with more than just my face.

When I was younger and much less secure in myself, I regularly compared every small aspect of myself to others. Somehow, in my own mind, I always seemed to come up lacking. It was like peering beneath my skin and finding nothing more than acne pits and scars.

One friend had a wonderfully infectious laugh that drew men to her in droves. From the day I first met her, I envied her that laugh. To my ears, my contained contralto laughter was OK, but it seemed to lack the same sparkling music I heard in my friend. As serious and contained as I was, I suppose the image I projected must have been much less light-hearted. And that laugh of mine certainly never seemed to attract the same crowds of male admirers.

In my gorgeous Danish sister-in-law, I saw a woman who was both sophisticated and elegant, as only a woman who has made a living as a model can be. Her beauty and poise intimidated me. Looking in my own mirror, I seemed to pale by comparison, always seeing extra pounds, hair not quite the right blonde or the most refined style, and clothing somewhat less than the most timeless fashions.

Yet another friend could sing with the voice of an angel. Like a diva at the Met, she would release her glorious soprano into the air for the sheer joy of raising her voice to the heavens. I, on the other hand, would sing so softly – if I sang at all – that it emerged as almost a whisper or a hum, background music and no more. Somehow when I was around her, I just knew that my voice was utterly toneless and without melody.

I spent so much time comparing myself to others, industriously searching for my failings, that I neglected to see two very important things – my own talents and the all-too-human imperfections and lives of those to whom I compared myself. Over time, though, I came to realize that each of these friends who had such God-given talents had endured the same ups and downs I had found in my life. Some had faced even greater challenges than I. The realization shifted my awareness.

I'm not sure when I changed. The transformation from self-critical to self-accepting was so gradual I didn't see what was happening. I just know that one day

Peeking Over the Edge

I woke up thankful for what I had made of myself and very grateful for a laugh that came from the heart, a style that was all my own, and a love of music that, while I might not ever be a singer, still put a song in my heart every day.

The thing about natural talents is they come so easily we sometimes fail to recognize them. When I first began to write, I believed it was something anyone could do. My closest friends quickly disabused me of that idea. That insight was a gift I will never forget.

Now, when I peer into that imaginary mirror, I see a woman who is entirely different from the young me. I see a woman who has learned to accept her own natural gifts and to overlook those she lacks. I can let other women be the singers and the models. Instead, I choose to remember the many times I have been given the gift of heartfelt compliments that carry the ringing tone of truth. I will accept those compliments as genuine. I will remember the women who have said they admire me for the talents that are uniquely mine. And I will hold their praise close to my heart to warm it in those rare times when I am tempted to give in to the chill of self criticism.

But for each of those women, the greatest gift I can return is to gently remind them to look to what they do most naturally and easily. That is where natural talents live. With coaxing, they will emerge into the light and they will bloom.

"A bird doesn't sing because it has an answer. It sings because it has a song."
Maya Angelou

☙

A Singing Heart, a Dancing Soul

Somewhere along the road that took me from carefree little girl to serious middle-aged woman, I lost something very important. I stopped singing and I stopped dancing. As my path wound through life's hills and valleys, the light heart of my childhood absorbed one judgment after another and one day, my song died. One by one, life added burdens to my youthful shoulders and the dancing ended.

If you watch children, every word is a song, every step a dance. Their prattling and laughing, skipping and hopping are natural expressions of simple joy. Somehow, as adults we forget that. Or we are taught restraint. Or perhaps we allow life's cares to still our voices and our bodies. For many of us, as the years pass, we learn to speak more softly for fear of being wrong. We learn to move more carefully for fear of taking a step out of an imaginary line. We learn to fear. That was me.

As a child, I sang and danced unselfconsciously, every movement and melody a simple expression of joy. I loved to talk and imagine, but it was music that touched everything I did. In my pre-Sesame Street world, I learned my ABCs by singing them. And in my games, "olly, olly, oxen free" had the rhythm of Broadway and was belted out with the vocal range of a pint-sized diva.

But in my first year of school, a single rebuke began quieting my song. Naturally gregarious and loving the new world of potential friends, I talked incessantly. That was my downfall. I was caught talking in class and the teacher scolded me. That unwelcome spotlight humiliated my sensitive heart and stilled my voice - just a little. As the years passed, with one small incident after another, it grew softer and quieter until the song became a whisper.

I remember the day my singing finally stopped. I was twenty-two. He was older, and the center of my living-alone, single-career-woman world. I believed I was in love. I know now he wasn't, but I didn't know it then. The evening had been just about perfect and as it ended, my heart sang. A melody flew, unbidden, to my lips. Softly, I sang my joy. I don't remember the song. I just remember how it stopped when the love of my life snarled, "What are you singing for? You can't carry a tune in a bucket!" At that moment, my song died, and the love began to wither. It was some time before the love affair stopped as well, but in time it did.

From that moment on, happiness and joy became emotions to be expressed quietly and never in song. Oh, I still loved music and the poetry of the truly gifted songwriter, but if melody escaped my lips it was only when I was alone with no one else to hear. My heart held the song close and very, very quiet for fear of the humiliation that could come at any moment should anyone hear what I knew was a horrible, off-key croaking. The singing child had learned to fear the judgment of others. The fear of singing had become complete.

Dancing was another matter entirely. I'm not sure exactly when I stopped dancing. It must have happened one step at a time because one day I was a child skipping through life without a care. The next time I looked, I was almost 40 and had stopped moving in every way. I think we stop dancing when the weight we carry in our hearts and minds and souls and yes, on our bodies, becomes too much to do more than plod through life, content to merely place one foot in front of the other, day after day after day.

I remember flashes through the years. Budding adolescence in grade school brought the intense social pressure of waiting to be asked to dance by a boy, any boy. Thinking, "Please someone ask me. Anyone?" In high school I somehow managed to acquire a "brainy" label. That reputation, coupled with my parents' opposition to teenage dating, was lethal to my social life and dancing never became an option. The dances themselves just never happened. By the time I started college, my desire to dance was so deeply buried I had forgotten it.

But then my life's tempo changed and like a powerful beat, the desire re-emerged. As a young woman on my own, I found a heady freedom in dancing and partying at the merest hint of an excuse. Eventually, in love once more, nothing thrilled my heart more than to move to music in the arms of the man I loved. The music itself mattered little. The touch, the movement, the feel of body against body was all. The dance became intimacy.

Still, much as we loved it, somewhere along the way, we did stop dancing. My feet slowed, my body grew heavier, and I allowed cares to become invisible, almost unconscious, burdens. Eventually, my feet stilled altogether, but like the singing, I missed dancing.

I believe, though, that song never completely leaves our hearts and dance never completely abandons our souls. You see, somehow here in mid-life, I have rediscovered both. I find myself seriously considering tango lessons at fifty-nine. Or maybe I'll try a little swing. I do know that whatever I do, my body will be moving, and my heart will be in full boogie! And the singing? Well, with the diva long gone, my song may not be as loud and enthusiastic as it was in my childhood. And I may never learn to be comfortable singing where I can be heard, but now when I do sing, it comes with full, conscious joy. In tune or out, it doesn't matter what I sing, only that I can. Often, my song finds its way to the page in words that I hope will resonate in other hearts. Perhaps that is how I was meant to sing all along.

Chapter 3

Joys & Magic & Bright Red Hearts… this little love of mine

☙

*"It's the heart, afraid of breaking, that never learns to dance.
It's the dream, afraid of waking, that never takes a chance.
It's the one who won't be taken, who cannot seem to give.
And the soul, afraid of dyin', that never learns to live."*

The Rose ~ lyrics by Amanda McBroom

"Love and magic have a great deal in common. They enrich the soul, delight the heart. And they both take practice."
Nora Roberts

ॐ

The Little Rose Bush That Could

One chilly February morning several months after settling into the house that we now call home, my husband spied an ad for beautiful bare-root tea rose bushes. Now, he knew next to nothing about how to plant bare root roses and he knew even less about how to care for the plant itself, but with hints of spring in the air that Sunday morning, he thought it was time to have a rose, so off he went to Home Depot's Garden Center. Hours later, he arrived home with his prize. Actually, it was little more than a stick with roots, but its tag promised a bush full of large, red roses — the rose of passion and love.

With a puzzled look, he held his stick out to me and asked, "What do I do now?" After I explained the planting process to him, he smiled and went off to prepare the planting hole and find a bucket where he could soak the roots. Later, with his rose lovingly settled into the somewhat stingy soil of our back yard, this retired engineer and former farmer began — much like a small child growing his first seedlings — to watch for signs of life. Every day.

Cathy Marley

And sure enough, in time buds began to form, then sprouts, then leaves. The day he spotted the first unopened bud was a cause for great excitement. He led me by the hand to his still-scrawny bush so I could see its almost-flower. I knew he was eagerly anticipating the pleasure of giving me huge bouquets of lovely long-stemmed red roses. Well, soon enough, that one small bud opened and revealed itself in all its beautiful <u>yellow</u> glory! We've never figured out exactly what happened with that bush. Was it mislabeled? Or did it just decide it was meant to be a yellow rose instead of red?

Regardless of what actually happened, that rose has become a source of endless fascination and a symbol of our life. Each day, year around, it produces one unique bloom. Sometimes that bloom is almost miniature, its size, like some days in a long marriage, almost insignificant. Other times the flower bursts forth with all the greatness of a florist's Valentine's Day offering. Some buds are a jumbled mass of petals. Others have just a bare few. Some days the petals are crisp and almost spiky. Other days they are smooth edged and have a placid aura about them. Usually, the flowers are a brilliant chrome yellow, but not always. Sometimes their color fades away until it is almost white by the time the flower opens fully. Other days, the petals are tinged with hints of red or the rose's very heart opens wide to reveal the loveliest coral color I have ever seen. Somehow, I think it's our rose's way of telling us that it could have been red if it had chosen to be, but it finds this life of endless variety a far more interesting way to live.

Peeking Over the Edge

What a fascinating symbol that rose bush has become between my husband and me! You see, if you study the meanings of rose colors, you will understand that the colors alone mirror our life. The red that sometimes peeks through represents the love and respect that are at the core of our world. The peach and coral that tinge the petals speak of desire, gratitude, appreciation, friendship and admiration – all qualities that have added depth to "us."

But the yellow is best of all. I believe it is truly the color that we were meant to have, for it is the color of joy, of gladness, of freedom. I believe that is the essence that remains when red's first fiery burst of passion passes, and two people intertwine their destinies into one.

Over the years, we have learned that cutting each day's offering helps to keep our rose blooming. And so, every day, my husband brings me my rose for the day. I find it incredibly romantic and touching. It reminds me of the romance that brought us together thirty years ago. It reminds me of all we have built together and all we have yet to do. It brings me joy and it touches my heart with love every day. It is a ritual that has become a most important part of our world. I know that wherever I am, my husband will find me and give me this small, ephemeral token of his continuing love. That is why I rarely cut the flowers myself.

From this remarkable little bush, no two roses are ever the same, just as no two days with this incredible man are ever the same. With their slightly spicy scent, my daily roses perfume my office and remind me of the romantic boy who hides within the heart of my gray-

Cathy Marley

haired husband. The roses he brings me have become a part of who we are. They twine through our days, the ritual surrounding them keeping our love close to our thoughts, their ever-changing character reminding us to keep the mystery alive.

"Age does not protect you from love, but love to some extent, does protect you from age."

Jeanne Moreau

☙

On Love and Valentines

When I was a little girl, Valentine's Day meant red satin hearts filled with mouth-watering chocolates from my father. But the rich candies, with their surprise centers were no match for the glory of that heart box with its shining satin, generous bow and blooming silk roses. I learned to believe that the bigger the heart, the fancier the box, the greater the love. At that age, love was a simple thing. But that changed once I started school.

Then, love's anticipation was built on shoe boxes dressed in crepe paper and adorned with paper doilies and painted flowers, their petals still emitting the waxy scent of Crayolas. Social acceptance came from a Valentine Box filled with child-sized envelopes and candy hearts saying, *Be Mine*. The more cards in the box, the more everyone liked you. The evening before Valentine's Day, I would spend hours matching just the right words for each classmate, careful to send secret messages of love to my favorite boy and girl friends in those mass-produced phrases. And I was convinced that every card I received was a coded message in return. I thought that was love. But I was wrong.

Cathy Marley

Time moved on, and love demanded more. No longer were children's valentines enough. Adolescent infatuations replaced paper doily hearts and candy sentiments. I wanted hand holding, long soulful looks, and cards hinting at undying love. Valentine's Day acquired an aura of innocent romance. I thought that was love. But I was wrong.

As time passed, commitment and passion gave romance a new dimension. The feelings associated with the holiday intensified - as did the tokens. Valentine's Day came to mean lacy black lingerie, red roses (for passion), intimate dinners for two and deeply meaningful cards. It meant searching for Mr. Right and kissing toads only to find they really were toads, not a prince in disguise among them. I abandoned innocent flirtations, replacing them with bodice-ripping passion. I thought that was love. But I was wrong.

But one day I kissed yet another toad in that long succession of two-legged amphibians and lo and behold, he was Mr. Right, Prince Charming with a crown invisible to most but faintly shimmering to *my* eyes. With him in my life, my view of Valentine's Day moved beyond the material. Today I know the satin hearts, romantic cards, lingerie and jewelry are nice, but they are not what matters to me. Love is far better when seen in a handmade construction paper heart from a child, a hug from a dear friend, a husband who empties the trash without prompting. My heart now sees love in everyday events and need not wait for a Valentine's Day to feel content. I know that is love.

> *"I don't want to get to the end of my life and find that I have lived just the length of it. I want to have lived the width of it as well."*
>
> Diane Ackerman

New Faces, Exotic Places

Growing up as a somewhat sheltered middle-class girl in a small town, I dreamed of travel to places exotic and foreign. By their very nature, Garland, Texas and my family dictated a very predictable life, but because I read voraciously, I lived in rich imagination. In my mind's eye, I could see a grown up me living an artist's life and drinking wine in Paris or zooming through the piazzas of Rome like Audrey Hepburn on a sporty Vespa motorbike. I knew endless stories about life in exciting places like New York, London and Athens, and without ever setting foot outside Texas, I could imagine riding camels in the Sahara or exploring the bazaars of Morocco. I thought for a while that perhaps I would someday work for the airlines, flying away every day to some thrilling and romantic city, seeing new faces and places with each turn of the earth. I craved an exotic life like a drunkard dreaming of 30-year old Scotch.

Somehow, I just knew that what I would find in other cities, other countries would be endlessly fascinating, expanding my horizons and experiences and making me over into the intriguing person I wanted to be. I suppose that woman was one formed in large part by the characters that populated my beloved books. You see, they were always well traveled, experienced, and often even world-weary.

World-weary. I think that was a term that defied my understanding. How, I wondered could anyone ever become weary of the endless variety to be found around the world? There was so much out there to see and to do! I couldn't imagine the excitement that would come with being able to lay my head on a different pillow every night, open my eyes to a new view every morning. What was wrong with people who complained about being tired of traveling? Couldn't they see all the adventure waiting for them if they could just escape the bonds of their boring, humdrum lives, lives like those my parents and their friends (and I of course) were leading?

As fate would have it, the day never came when my daily existence could be travel and the thrill of flying. Instead, much like my parents before me, I found myself taking jobs because they were available or paid well, not because they offered exotic adventure. Still, the dream persisted, and I found myself experiencing little thrills of "what-ifs." What if I could work on a cruise ship? What if I could find a job that required travel? What if I became a secretary in an embassy? I even considered moving to Australia where I heard they were paying to have Americans relocate. Year after year, I dreamed my "what-ifs," always looking for ways to satisfy that decades-old wanderlust.

Sometimes I found brief moments of satisfaction in short vacations. I discovered that I could make my own travel arrangements and find myself on a plane to somewhere. So what if it was only a trip to Texas to visit my aunt? At least I was flying away! Looking back at those carefree years, I know I was traveling more than most single women. After all, I had been to Hawaii – several times. So what if it was only to visit my sister? But, I wanted more.

Eventually, I married a man who traveled often and through him I saw those foreign lands - still vicariously, but closer than they had been in my beloved books. In meeting his customers, I met people who lived in those places I had only read about or seen in my dreams. Hearing his stories when he returned home, I experienced something more than what I had read. I could almost taste the air and hear the music of foreign lands. Occasionally, I was actually able to travel with him and I treasured those times as a small fulfillment of my long-held dreams.

One day, I finally visited Paris and my heart soared with the excitement of that dream realized. The artist's life there was not meant for me to have, but on one sunny day in August, I did drink wine and dine at a street café in Paris. As I grew older, my life became more flexible and I took the time to indulge my life-long fantasies of exploration. Paris was followed in time by Puerto Vallarta and Baja and Panama and Costa Rica. Then there was Tahiti where I walked the sands in Gauguin's footsteps and breathed the delicious island aromas that always seemed to lurk just beneath the surface of the oils he laid down on canvas.

I suppose some people – maybe even the little girl I once was – would say that I am better traveled than many in this world. I know I have seen places and peoples my own mother and grandmother never hoped to see. I know too that I will never stop traveling, but I no longer crave the excitement and the exotic life for my day-to-day existence. I still enjoy learning and experiencing new places and people, but I have finally come to understand how someone can grow world-weary. Nothing ever compares to the joy of coming home.

You see, for me travel without the threads tying me back to the home I love is meaningless, and new experiences are hollow without someone I love to share them with. I have discovered that the true joy in travel is the shared experience and the returning home to the familiar. The memories of travels add but a small part to life's richness. All too often, those memories fade with time. My cats curled in my lap, the familiar hollows of my own bed, a long telephone talk with a friend, morning coffee and the local paper across the table from my husband, these are the things that imprint themselves upon my heart and make my life full. These are the memories that endure.

"Eat what you don't like fast, and linger over the ice cream sundaes in life."
        Marilyn vos Savant

Someday Is Today

For more than half my life, I have lived with the same man. The pattern of our lives moves in an intricate dance, as we twirl together, apart, around and back together, much like lead dancers weaving our way through a crowded troupe, always finding one another again. We eat, sleep, dream, and dress together. I retire for the night and he is there, a solid presence of love beside me. I wake and still he is there, breathing the same air. We rise, and each go our own way, dealing with the minutiae of life. But still our paths touch in that random dance that keeps us always aware, one of the other. It is a life that is as familiar to me as the hand at the end of my arm.

Ours is not a life of dependence. Rather, the "we" that we are is built of two strong, whole beings who each become so much more in the presence of the other. It is a relationship built on a triangle-strong foundation of friendship, respect and love. He celebrates my strengths, as I do his. I turn to him as my rock of sanity in a sometimes insane world, as he does me. I have become self-assured and somewhat assertive over the years because he believes I can. Sometimes I know he believes in me even more than I believe in myself. This is a man who has woven himself into the very fabric of my soul. I cannot imagine life without him.

And yet over this last year, that almost happened. It made us both realize that now is the only time that ever matters in life. What happened yesterday is gone. To spend energy regretting past mistakes or to live in past glories is to live in the past. The past is a time that holds no mystery. We know how that story ends. It ends in today. To focus only on tomorrow is equally pointless. If we live only for what will happen someday, how easily we may miss the joys of today!

For thirty-two years, we have linked arms and fixed our eyes firmly on "someday." Many of those years were a struggle as we pulled together, working – always working. Our goal was security and comfort to sustain us in our later years and we knew that if we only worked hard enough, the goal would be ours. Always, we would reassure one another that the effort was worthwhile. Someday, we would fill our plates with the fruits of our labor and eat our fill. We knew that someday would come, well someday.

Someday we would travel together just for the fun of it. Someday, we would allow ourselves time to just do nothing if we chose. Someday, we would play games together rather than sit mesmerized in front of a mindless television. Someday, we would sit quietly and read together, not speaking, just spending companionable time with books and each other. Someday, we would stop industriously accumulating security and learn to play. Someday, we would relax and enjoy life. Someday.

Peeking Over the Edge

Well now we know that someday is today. Nothing brings that home more than facing a tomorrow of solitude. Almost losing half of my world was a sobering experience. Suddenly, I see the things I may never be able to do if I don't do them now. And so, now we are doing, not delaying. Holding hands, talking quietly, kissing, cuddling and laughing with one another, our dance has become more waltz than *pas-de-deux*. Today, we make time to enjoy each other, whatever form that may take. Today, we give ourselves permission to spend the time and the money to do the things we were saving for tomorrow. Today, we live. Someday has finally come.

"Nothing you do for children is ever wasted. They seem not to notice us, hovering, averting our eyes, and they seldom offer thanks, but what we do for them is never wasted."
                                   Garrison Keillor

Mothers and Daughters

Everyone knows there's something very special about the connection between a mother and a daughter. I think in some ways I have been more fortunate than many mothers who, having raised their children from infancy, must eventually experience the sometimes devastating emotional wrench that comes with the maturing of their baby and the severing of apron strings.

My daughter came to me when I married her father. She was twelve and I was twenty-seven, so our relationship began at a point somewhat beyond her most formative years. Even so, we have spent a lifetime building understanding and compassion for one another.

Now, with me nearing sixty and Dennie just turned forty-five, I can say that we have safely made the transition from parent-child to adult-adult. Talking as only adults will talk with one another, our age differences have become nonexistent.

Cathy Marley

Today we talked of life and death, and the deep love we as women feel for our children and our families. We explored what it means to be a stepparent and how it feels to be a stepchild. We have each experienced both sides of that equation.

With her first husband, this daughter of my heart became a young stepmother herself. After his untimely death, she eventually remarried and became a stepmother again. When she did, her son became a stepchild in his own right and, unlike me, she experienced the divided heart that comes with loving someone who is stepparent to your own child.

Having lost my own mother when I was twelve, I became a stepchild at thirteen. I don't know if that experience gave me any particular empathy for the plight of my own three stepchildren, but I know it gives us a common ground and perhaps a slightly deeper understanding of one another.

Perhaps that is why Dennie so touched my heart when she told me that I have truly been a mother to her, that she will always choose to be a part of my life. I suppose a small fear lurked deep down inside that I would lose her if I ever lost her father. The tears quickened in my eyes when I realized that will never happen. I am so incredibly humbled to know I will always have a place in the heart of this wondrous woman.

A friend of mine was recently preparing to send her college freshman daughter across the country to school for the first time. She told me it was, as was to be expected, an emotional wrench for them both. But then she acknowledged something very profound. She told me she could sense their relationship undergoing a significant change. They were spending time together as two women who enjoyed each other's company, not purely as mother and daughter.

I think that's what my relationship with my own daughter has become. We respect each other for the powerful, loving, sensitive women we both are. Right now, she is going through unbearable stresses in her life and as she adjusts to middle age, she sees the hurdles she has been forced to leap on her way there. But she also suffers from the worry of the hurdles she sees ahead. My heart aches with the need to help, to hurl those obstacles aside for her. I want to protect her from it all, but I know that is something I cannot and should not do. It would be such a terrible disservice to her. I know she must continue to grow through her own challenges, as did I.

They say that a butterfly must break free of its cocoon on its own, that if you help it into the world, its wings will never be strong enough for it to fly. I know that. I have experienced it for myself. But still I pray for my daughter's life to ease, for her growth to come without struggle. After all, that's what a mother does, isn't it?

"Gratitude unlocks the fullness of life. It turns what we have into enough, and more. It turns denial into acceptance, chaos to order, confusion to clarity. It can turn a meal into a feast, a house into a home, a stranger into a friend. Gratitude makes sense of our past, brings peace for today, and creates a vision for tomorrow."
                                            Melody Beattie

Rich Girl, Poor Girl and Simple Abundance

I grew up in a middle-class home. We were neither rich nor poor, merely comfortable. As a child, I never received *everything* I wanted, but I was rarely denied the things I desired most. As many children are wont to do, though, I tended to focus on the things I did not have and so grew up envying those I thought had so much more than I did.

Nowhere did I feel that comparison more than when I visited my two closest cousins, Betty Jean and Jerry Don.

Betty lived in a large house with wall-to-wall carpeting and central air conditioning. In the 1950s, both were luxuries far beyond my family's limited means. We softened our hardwood floors with rugs and cooled the air with open windows. Betty had a white

French provincial bedroom set and doll furniture to match. By comparison, my room's mahogany bed, lilac walls and hand-quilted spread felt sadly lacking to me. I would look at her many dolls and dancing lessons and feel much like the "poor" cousin. I never thought about how much, only child that she was, she envied me my older sister and younger brother.

In some oddball twist of logic, I found a certain romance in the creaking wood floors and flimsy screen doors of Jerry's simple farm home. I can still hear the loud rattle of those doors banging shut behind me when I passed through their solitary barrier to the bare dirt yard. Those doors, portals as they were to crawdad fishing holes, barnyard cats, nearby railroad tracks and rural stores with grape Nehi dispensers, were country-bred music to my city-tuned ears. I thought it terribly unfair that Jerry lived where he had such ready access to the adventures promised by cotton fields and ponds and open spaces. I envied his entire family the thrill of bathing, one after the other, in a washtub in the kitchen and perching above what seemed a deep and slightly frightening dark hole in an outhouse when they needed a toilet. I never realized that while I played, they all had the responsibility of daily chores just to survive on that farm. I never knew they viewed me as the "rich" city cousin.

Through my teens and into early womanhood, I studied the lifestyle, manners and graces of those I perceived, by virtue of their material wealth, to be my betters. I studied magazines and movies with the devoted concentration of an acolyte studying for the priesthood. At every turn, I could see only the "perfection" and abundance enjoyed by the rest of the world, but I could never see my own. The more I observed, the more I tried to imitate, in whatever way I could, the lifestyles I so admired. I became a master at copying on a budget. I learned to sew so I could duplicate the styles I saw in magazines such as *Mademoiselle* and *Vogue*. Through poring over every article about turning other people's trash into interior design masterpieces, I mastered a "shabby chic" decorating style long before it even had a name.

Well, as time went on, I was able to afford more and more "things," material manifestations of the abundance I thought I had missed. Parties, social occasions and model homes became dangerous traps for me. Parties meant a completely new outfit whether I could afford it or not. If I had a date, I would often insist on something new to wear even if the occasion was as simple as dinner and a movie with a long-time boyfriend. Beautifully decorated homes left me unable to rest until I had done something to polish my own apartment. One purchase at a time, I crept closer and closer to becoming an out of control shop-a-holic. The habit escalated for years.

But one day well into my middle age, I realized that all the "things" I had accumulated weren't giving me the feeling of wealth, the satisfaction I had expected from them. Buying more simply was not the answer to feelings of inadequacy. That was a practice rooted in both emotional poverty and insecurity. Gradually, my perspective began to shift to one of abundance. Over time, I learned to gauge my own abundance by the fullness of my heart rather than my possessions. Perhaps it was through a new-found measure of maturity I became more aware of the gifts I had in my life.

I discovered that "rich" people aren't always rich and "poor" people aren't always poor. True abundance, rather, comes from deep inside the soul. It is irrevocably linked with appreciation of the small joys of life - with giving and receiving freely - with love of family and friends - with appreciation of life as it is right now! I could have been immensely wealthy, but what I have is so much better. I am content with the course my life has taken. I am immeasurably rich in family and friends, and I live in a world filled with an abundance of beauty - mine for the taking whenever I want. Life is good, and I am forever grateful.

"If you ask me what I came to do in this world ... I am here to live out loud."
                                       Emile Zola

☙

Bungee

I collect frogs. Why is not particularly pertinent here, nor is the size or variety of the collection. What does matter is the most recent addition - "Bungee Frog." Bungee hangs from my ceiling, suspended in mid-leap from a golden bungee line just beginning to recoil. Now, I've never had an overwhelming desire to jump from a bridge with a bungee cord tied to my ankles. The mere idea of leaping into space tethered to one small breakable line terrifies me. Even so, I must say this frog brings a smile to my face and inspires me every time I see him. When I first spotted him in a Sedona art gallery, I screamed with delight and knew I <u>had</u> to have this frog!

With his arms (or is it legs?) outstretched wide and his eyes goggling in excitement, Bungee is gleefully grinning from ear to ear as he eagerly leaps into the unknown. In his exuberance, I can see a being totally embracing life. Rather than just creating a whimsical hanging sculpture, the artist has created a "snapshot" of zest for living.

In Bungee, I can see faith - a total confidence that his safety line will always be strong, steady, and dependable. I can see risk with an understanding that it gives zest to life and leads to the greatest rewards. I can see the thrill of that adrenaline rush that comes from conquering fears. Most of all, I can see joy. The joy of life! Life, with its beginnings (that first leap out into space) and its endings (that heart-stopping moment when we reach the end of the bungee), its suspense (will the life line hold?), and its thrills (the complete exhilaration of the ride).

Bungee *is* an inspiration to me. He hangs just inside my front door where I am reminded, anytime I pass, that life has so much more flavor when I conquer my fears and throw my arms open wide to all of life. I may not ever take such a huge leap into the unknown as Bungee, but I do believe I can live every bit as completely. That is a life worth living!

"We're conditioned to think that our lives revolve around great moments. But great moments often catch us unaware – beautifully wrapped in what others may consider a small one."
                                          Kent Nerburn

ఌ

The Christmas Angel

As I grow older, it seems that the magic of the Holidays becomes ever more elusive and the Christmas Spirit seems to come later with each passing year. Perhaps, with years of repetition, I've become a harsher critic of what constitutes enchantment. I think I've allowed the "responsibilities" of the season to overshadow the potential for joy and lightness of spirit. Sometimes I completely lose sight of why I have always loved the Holiday season.

Inevitably, though, something happens to spark the warmth and open my eyes to the joy around me. I think of that something as a tiny Christmas angel who watches out for those of us in danger of becoming Scrooges. She tosses reminders of the magic before us like stardust and hopes that we will only *look*.

She gives us the rapt faces of young children gazing in awe at a simple mall Santa Claus. Her delicate touch opens our eyes to the breathtaking beauty of ordinary homes magically transformed by hundreds of tiny lights. Tinkling Salvation Army bells are her reminder that this is truly a season of unconditional giving. She fills our homes with the scents of the season - cinnamon, pine, bayberry, baking cookies, and <u>chocolate</u>! With her help, firelight, tree lights and candle glow touch our tired eyes and reach our hearts. Everywhere we turn, she shows us examples of love, forgiveness, compassion, magic, and joy.

I believe my Christmas angel is the spirit of all that is good within us. Whatever your faith, my wish for you is that she will reach your heart when you need her and that you never lose sight of the magic.

"Every day brings a chance for you to draw in a breath, kick off your shoes, and dance."

Oprah Winfrey

൪

Grow Up!

When was the last time you heard, "Why don't you grow up?" A friend of mine, well into her forties and a mother herself, recently heard those very words from her own mother. It seems the mother accused her daughter of wanting to be a kid all her life. Now I ask, "What's wrong with that?"

Why is it that we treasure in children what we deny our adult selves? In fact, those very qualities that make children so endearing are all too often considered irresponsible in grown-ups. Perhaps our lives would be happier and far more content if we all tried to be <u>more</u> child-like! The things we love about children are the very qualities that can keep us young no matter how many years we carry on our body.

I look at children and see small beings whose enthusiasm and genuine zest for living inspire me to regain my sense of wonder. For them, each moment brings some exciting new adventure to be savored and investigated. They see everything with the fresh eyes of the very young. Puddles and puppies, stars, fireflies, bubbles, kites, ants, and even elephants - all stir a child's sense of wonder and curiosity. Most every experience holds promise of entertainment. From my somewhat jaded perspective of fifty-eight years, I think it must be so very exciting to embrace each moment as a chance to search for the new rather than the expected!

I think what I love most about children, though, is their uncomplicated sense of fun. They laugh easily and long at some of the silliest things! Corny jokes, marshmallow fights, and even tickles can set off gales of uncontrollable giggles and pleas for more. Somehow children, always ready to laugh and play, do not take themselves or their world too seriously. It's only as we build walls of self-importance that we learn to do that.

So, I think my friend is right. I don't want to be a "grownup." I'd much rather view the world as a constantly new experience, expecting some grand adventure to be lurking just around the next corner and facing my challenges with enthusiasm and curiosity. And I think maybe a giggle and a hug a day will really be fun too, don't you?

"Life is meant to be lived. Enjoy! Laughing helps. It's like jogging on the inside."
                                    Author Unknown

❦

Magical Fifty

It was my fiftieth birthday. Like most people reaching the half-century mark, I felt the occasion deserved some measure of celebration. I wanted to dance and sing and kick up my heels in joy, but even at that age, I was still hesitant to ask for what I really wanted. In very typical male fashion, my ever-thoughtful husband presented me with several options for marking the occasion. He suggested a huge party with all our friends and acquaintances and even offered to arrange it himself. On the other hand, if I would rather have a quiet celebration with just the two of us over a quiet dinner, I had only to ask. Or, maybe the lights and excitement of Las Vegas? Just make the reservations.

Well, in my most secret fantasies, I was really hoping someone would - just this once - surprise me. Over my lifetime I had been a part of the planning for so many surprise parties with their mystery, intrigue, and depth of feeling that I yearned for that special attention that said, "I want to celebrate your life. I'll do all the planning - with the help of good friends. And we'll really keep the secret. The surprise is our gift to you."

Of course, a surprise party was never a real option. After all, a surprise isn't much of a surprise if you have to suggest it yourself. Our favorite Vegas hotel was booked solid for the two months around my birthday, so bright lights, gambling and glitzy shows were out. And somehow I knew that if I asked for the big party, I wouldn't be able to resist planning and executing my own celebration.

No, none of the obvious choices seemed to be quite right for leaping into the second half of my life. For weeks I put off a decision, still hoping someone would sneak that surprise in on me but knowing better. I suppose it really came down to one simple decision. You see, I love planning parties for other people and I love having parties just because, but this time I just did not want to be the one to plan my own celebration. I think it would have been anti-climactic. And so, I balked. And I delayed.

Then, one day, a mere two weeks before the fateful day, I chanced upon an advertisement for . . . Disneyland! Suddenly, everything fell into place. It was the Magic Kingdom! How could I ever feel old if I was rubbing elbows with laughing, running children, Snow White and Mickey Mouse? Disneyland was a place where I could celebrate with all my heart and release every thought of being over the hill the minute it wandered into my consciousness! Maybe I could even be a kid again for a little while. Oh, I knew it would be just the two of us, but we would be surrounded by

Peeking Over the Edge

wonder and joy. And, like two very large and well-wrinkled children, we would be playing our hearts out.

This was a party I didn't mind planning. Of course, the little girl in me still wanted the balloons, cake, presents, and hordes of friends, but in the absence of that big surprise party, I realized that I could make my own party after all. I <u>could</u> still be a kid, even at fifty! Even more importantly, I realized I didn't need a big crowd and a "surprise!" to feel special. By doing something completely different, something I <u>really</u> wanted to do, I could create my own magic and mystery with a little help from the ageless population of the Magic Kingdom.

When my birthday weekend arrived, we found ourselves at a Holiday Inn nestled in the skirts of Disneyland. For two days, we did exactly what *I* wanted to do. We arrived early and stayed late. We rode every ride we wanted, even the scary ones! We ate junk food during the day and room service at night. I screamed on the roller coasters and gasped in wide-eyed wonder as we flew in outer space and rode a submarine beneath the "ocean." A pounding heart and racing blood sent zings sparking through my body from one moment to the next and I thrived on the adrenaline coursing through my system! It felt good!

Immersing myself, at fifty, in a place designed for "children of all ages," I learned to play again. I remembered how to laugh! And, I forgot the sneaky little aches and pains that had gradually crept up on me over the years. For two days, the child in me came out to play and when I left, I went with a lighter heart, a more ready smile, and an eager anticipation of the years

Cathy Marley

yet to come. That brief visit to childhood's enchantment reminded me that life does not need to be a long, slow slide into old age. Instead, in embracing play and laughter, I can live the rest of my years with a heart that will always be young. That was the true magic.

"The roses, the lovely notes, the dining and dancing are all welcome and splendid. But when the Godiva is gone, the gift of real love is having someone who'll go the distance with you. Someone who, when the wedding day limo breaks down, is willing to share a seat on the bus."

Oprah Winfrey,
O Magazine, February 2004

Heroes, Heroines and Bodice Rippers

I rarely allow myself the luxury of reading romance novels, especially "bodice rippers." You know. They're the ones whose heroines are beautiful, strong willed and intelligent with the body of a goddess and flowing masses of golden or fiery or raven curls. The heroes are always tall, ruggedly handsome and immensely wealthy with no real need to work. They have sculpted, powerful bodies, warm, bedroom eyes, and smiles that alternate between heart-meltingly lazy and sardonic.

In the perfect world of the romance novel, the heroine faces some peril from which only our hero can rescue her. He tries to resist her charms, but she is irresistible. She defies his power but is always overcome by the protection his strong will imposes on her. Their love-hate relationship becomes increasingly stormy as they angrily battle the passions that seem to boil to the surface with every line of the book. Finally, in a pulse-pounding conclusion, they give in to all they've been resisting, and their conflict is magically resolved. Like a fairy tale, everyone lives happily ever after thanks to unending passion, all-consuming love and, of course, limitless wealth and servants.

I love those books, predictable as they may be. They tap into every one of the fantasies I have nurtured from the first moment I knew there was a difference between little boys and little girls. Immersed in the story, I dream. I dream of romance and its partner – passion. I dream of desire beyond reason. I dream of things I would never want in saner moments. I dream.

Oh, how dangerous those books are for me! Always, I turn the last page and find myself feeling vaguely dissatisfied. The cover closed, I look at my life and see a house in the suburbs with no servants to cook and clean. I look in the mirror and see no perfect body or cascading waves of irresistibly sexy hair. I see jeans and sweatshirts rather than satins, pearls, and tuxedoes. I see bills to pay and all the responsibilities of everyday life. I see a husband whose hair is somewhat less than full and dark and whose body is somewhat less than sculpted. Finally, I see no passionate embraces or heart-pounding sex.

My deepest heart shouts, "I *want* to be the heroine! I want my husband to be the hero! I want to be so deeply desired that I am consumed with passion, melting kisses, and sexual fireworks." Perhaps that's why the bodice ripper novels are so immensely popular. The authors merely write our deepest fantasies.

Peeking Over the Edge

And how unrealistic those fantasies are! I know I'll never be that perfect heroine, but to my husband I am - almost. He'll never be that perfect hero, but to me he is - almost. He's the mate I chose, not because he's tall, dark and handsome, but because he's warm, caring and always here when I need him, his eyes shining with a love that transforms him into a towering hero. We may no longer feel the rampaging passions of the romance novel, but once we did. I treasure those memories, but now, thirty-two years later, I value our easy intimacy even more. The brief, hot flashes of passion come farther and farther apart. With those fires banked, we have become more like the long-married parents of the hero or the heroine - fitting comfortably together and loving each other for the long term. But then, maybe that's where the hero and heroine will be in thirty-two years too.

Chapter 4

You & Me Together ...
this little world of mine

"Take your place on The Great Mandella
As it moves through your brief moment of time.
Win or lose now you must choose now
And if you lose you've only wasted your life."

The Great Mandella ~ lyrics by Albert Grossman,
Mary Travers &Peter Yarrow

"Many people live in great turmoil because they are taught that they should 'love thy neighbor' but cannot resolve how to love their neighbor when he does something they don't like or don't feel is right. To obtain peace of mind, one must love his fellow man unconditionally. However, loving him does not necessarily mean that you must like what he does. One must learn to separate the person from the act."

Thomas D. Willhite
Living Synergistically

○∂

I Believe in One World

I believe no matter how divided or angry the peoples of this planet become, we are still only one world. Like islands firmly planted on a common sea floor, we are all linked to one another. No matter how rich or poor the islands may be above the waterline, they are the same soil below. And no matter how different we may appear to be from others, we are, at heart, one.

I was raised by a father that many people today would consider to be a bigot. A product of the south and World War II, he learned prejudice from a world that accepted it as truth and from a war that divided races. He carried many of those misguided beliefs with him to his grave. And he did his best to pass them along to my sister, my brother and me. I know he believed it was his duty as a father to teach us those values, no matter how misguided they may have been. It was a form of protection – protection for himself as much as for us. It was also all he knew.

But I have learned a different reality. I have learned that the color of skin or shape of eye or size or gender or religious belief or foreign birth or disability does not make the person. In reality, these are merely details that are all little more than surface. As a part of who we are, they are important details, but our common ground is so much more important. In our basic humanity, there is very little difference between us.

I see that commonality in my friends Danette and Chris, both well along in their pregnancies. What touches my soul is the joy of motherhood that shines equally on Danette's black face and Chris' white one. The unconditional love that comes with motherhood transcends their differences and unites them in a common bond.

I watch the news and I see a woman covered head to toe in her sad black burka, wailing her grief to the heavens over a lost loved one. Is her anguish any greater or less than that of a woman in a more modern, westernized society? I think not. Grief is humanity at its saddest. It transports us all to a shared space.

Human emotions know no boundaries of country. Regardless of race or nationality or core beliefs, at some time each of us experiences grief and love, peace and pain. We cry when we hurt. We laugh when we are joyous. Human feelings need no words. They are a common language for us all.

As a little girl growing up in a strictly segregated 1950s Texas, I was taught that much of the world was inferior to me. I learned all the slurs and knowing no better, used them often. I learned to believe that color or religious belief or nationality was a measure of the person. Fortunately, with exposure what we learn can sometimes be unlearned.

For me, the unlearning began when I reached high school and met Leon Jordan and Roosevelt Woods, two gifted teachers and both men of color. My first days in sophomore biology and art were a shock to my ingrained sense of righteous prejudice. But as the days passed, I became entranced by the knowledge these two men were sharing. Never did I hear reference to our differences. I heard only the truths of great art and the uncompromising science of biology.

By the time the year ended, I was no longer conscious of either man's color. I saw only the person inside. Somewhere in that year, I had learned to respect each man for his intelligence, his humor, his dignity, his humanity. Those two remarkable men taught me so much more than high school art and biology. They taught me tolerance. That began a transformation that has lasted a lifetime.

Now, after more than fifty years of observing the world and the people in it, I know that when a child starves in a war-torn Nigeria, I become a little bit hungrier in my own soul. When a mother grieves a son lost to war, we all feel the sadness in our own hearts.

Cathy Marley

When a terrorist takes innocents in a fiery blast of hatred, the world and all the people in it loses a measure of humanity.

Chaos theory suggests that the whisper of a butterfly's wings in the rain forest can echo across time and space, affecting weather in the deepest Sahara. I have learned to trust that much like the Butterfly Effect, what I do and believe affects my family, my neighbor, my country, and in some small measure, every other person in the world. I know that when the artificial boundaries forming our biases are removed, we are in truth, one world.

"I know in my heart that man is good. That what is right will always eventually triumph. And there's purpose and worth to each and every life."
Ronald Reagan

Winged People in Feather Coats

In my house is a large picture window that faces the street. Even though we are close to the occasional traffic of cars and passers-by, it has something of a garden feel to it, thanks to lush trees, bushes and a small waterfall we built some years back. Beside the pond is a water dish we keep filled for the birds. Every morning (at least until the pigeons become gluttons) we sprinkle seed for their daily meals. I have found that observing these birds is much like reading the morning newspaper. They each represent a microcosm of our human society.

If you observe the different species of birds carefully, you'll see that, like small winged people in feather coats, many of their actions are much like our own. They're all birds, but they each deal with life in a different way. Some are aggressive, some sweet and shy. Others are cocky and boastful. Still other birds just live from moment to moment and sing for the sheer joy of life. Are we not much the same?

Sometimes, watching the birds is a little like watching cop shows on television. The thrashers are like juvenile misfits, gang members if you will, purposely dashing headlong into whatever group happens to be going about a law-abiding life. They chase everyone away with their brash aggressiveness. Starlings, much like their criminal human counterparts, are the lazy thieves of the bird world, readily stealing nests from others rather than exert the energy to build their own. Both birds storm through life with little concern for anything but their own needs.

Thrashers and starlings, I think, are in the minority, just as the criminal element is an exception in our world. Because they make such a stir, we notice them, and we comment on their actions. Their attitude is what you notice first. It so overshadows the cheerful, curious sparrows and the sweet but very average minded doves. And of course, it is the total opposite of the quail who are responsible little beings that take family life very seriously. Much like Joe and Jane Average Citizen, they comfortably wear the mantle of their family duties, male and female alike becoming fearless when their children are threatened. Today I watched a young male perched high on a rock, waiting to eat and attentively guarding his bride as she had her evening meal first. It was a testament to the commitment these birds make to one another when they mate for life.

Over the years I have seen war as hummingbirds battle over territory, community judgment in courts of mynahs deciding the fate of a wrongdoer, and love every spring in the puffed posturing and romantic cooing of doves seeking mates. It is all so very human.

Somehow, all the birds seem to get by in their own way. Each appears to respect the nature of the

Peeking Over the Edge

others. Perhaps the quail and the dove recognize the futility of trying to be like a thrasher. Perhaps the thrasher is not really a bully, but simply a being whose aggression is little more than protective posturing. I like to believe each lives true to its own nature but is something more for being a part of the whole. That little something more is the connection of understanding and acceptance that, as it does for the birds, also binds humans together in the end. It is our very difference from one another that makes us, like the birds, so endlessly fascinating.

"Acknowledge each day the contributions you make – a smile, the flowers in your yard, a job well done, a kind word given to another. Though seemingly small, these are the things that make the world beautiful."

Thomas D. Willhite
The Book of Power

ॐ

Smile!

One deliciously balmy spring afternoon last week, as I was driving from one "important" meeting to another, I noticed something as rare as a rainbow in Phoenix. I drove past a woman who was walking down the street all alone, her only companion a broad, glowing smile. She was a rather plain woman in a rough part of town and from the way she was dressed, I suspect she may have been homeless. But there was that smile. It transformed her face into something so luminous I simply had to stare. As far as I could tell, there was no *reason* for that smile - it just was. What caught my attention was the rarity of seeing anyone smiling to themselves with such obvious joy!

I could make up a story about that woman and why she was smiling, but the woman was not the story. It was the smile. Looking at her, I realized that all too often, I stride purposefully through life, so intent on a goal and so focused on achieving it that I miss the small joys and wonders that fill the world. I forget to smell roses and so miss the moment of reawakened memory their perfume usually evokes in my heart. I overlook the cooing and posing of doves courting and so miss the laughter their uncanny imitations of teen-age Don Juans always bring to my lips. In my purposefulness, the sun provides light, but its comforting warmth fails to penetrate beyond my skin to my heart. Music becomes background rather than a lift for my spirits. In short, I sometimes take myself so seriously that I forget to smile at life!

    I can't help but wonder - what is there to be so serious about? True, we all have to deal with "the icky stuff" on occasion, but facing life with a smile in our hearts and on our faces certainly makes the tough times easier to handle. What would happen if people started wearing smiles - just because?! Do you suppose the world might become a happier place? I know the pessimists out there will cry "Yeah, but ... What about war, death, disease, abuse, etc.?" Well, those things certainly won't go away by themselves, and smiling more may not be the solution, but can it hurt?

    I think I might try being like the woman I saw last week. Maybe the two of us will start a new trend! After all, they say a smile is infectious. Pass it on.

"Life is a short walk. There is so little time and so much living to achieve."
                                   John Oliver Killens

ಌ

First Day, Last Day

There is an old saying that reminds us "Today is the first day of the rest of your life." If we believe the saying, no matter how old we are, we can look at our future as filled with unlimited possibilities. But even better, knowing it allows us to shake off the dust of past mistakes and stride confidently into the future, unfettered by the past. What a wonderful way to view the future!

I try to remember, though, that there is another side to the saying which most of us tend to forget. If today is the first day of the rest of my life, it could also be the last. Never is this brought home more strongly than in the loss, through either death or alienation, of a cherished friend or relation.

In focusing on work, or paying my bills, or what to fix for dinner, or cleaning the house, or any of my daily multitude of obligations, I sometimes lose sight of the connections that so enrich my life. It is easy to forget saying "I love you" or to listen with only half my attention when my children call. I can become too busy to visit quietly with a friend and truly hear what her heart is saying. I put off calling a sister or a father, lightly believing I will do it tomorrow. And, somehow, troubled relationships stay un-mended. Until sometimes, it's too late.

Because today *could* be the last day of my life, or of my family's, or my friends', I keep my relationships as clean as I can. Somehow, from the perspective of an uncertain future, differences lose their power and tolerance tempered with patience becomes a much more natural way of life. I have found it is critical to my peace of mind that I forgive slights, remember to say "I love you" to those I cherish, give freely of myself, and live life as fully as I can - every day, every moment!

Chapter 5

Today, Tomorrow & For Always… this little legacy of mine

*"Now, I'm not countin' on riches or fame to make my mark
The best I can do is touch someone and hope they feel my spark
And maybe add a little sunlight where no sun ever shines,
'Cause I gotta be more than just two lines in the Oklahoma City Times"*

Oklahoma City Times ~ lyrics by Paul Hampton

"If we listened to our intellect, we'd never have a love affair, we'd never have a friendship, we'd never go into business, because we'd be cynical. Well, that's nonsense. You've got to jump off cliffs all the time and build your wings on the way down."

          Ray Bradbury

Peeking Over the Edge

For the first forty or more years of my life, I often wondered what I'd be when I grew up. That was a big question, since the princess jobs were all filled. But I really wasn't worried since I knew I had plenty of time to decide. After all, I was young, and life was one merry party after another. And so, I drifted with the flow, finding it easier to follow the path of least resistance as I accepted the immediate gratification of a weekly paycheck over the delayed reward of a degree and a career. Gravid with untapped potential, my future stretched before me. But what I didn't notice as I danced forward were the opportunities I was carelessly tossing behind me like discarded toys that have lost a child's interest.

One day, I found myself somewhere in middle age, perched firmly near the top of a hill. I thought to myself, *I've never noticed this hill before*. The climb up had been so gradual that I had never felt it. But looking at my hill, I noticed that it was, in reality, a pretty big one and that I had climbed a rather long way.

I felt much like those cowboys in the old western movies. You know the ones. Often, when they reach the pass, they're running *from* something at the same time they're running *to* something. Even though they have a pretty good idea of what lies ahead, they still climb to the top of the hill and, keeping a low profile, peek over to cautiously check the other side. Sometimes as they lie there they're surprised - not by the ambush they are expecting to be lying in wait before them, but by the posse they forgot was nipping at their heels.

Well, on that lovely day in my middle age, I slipped my fingers over the edge then lifted my head and carefully peeked over. Like the cowboy, I was caught off guard. But unlike the cowboy, I was surprised by what I saw in both directions.

Behind me, I saw the pearls of missed opportunities and dreams lying inert and dulled in lush grasses of complacency. Oh, I had no serious regrets for that first half of my life. It had its share of successes that I could measure in a loving family, a comfortable home and financial security. Those joys greened the hillside that was my past, but on close inspection I could barely find "me."

I looked, and way back at the beginning of the hill was a small creative girl bubbling over with dreams of glory. Closer still was a young college student who chose the practicality of mathematics over her passion for literature and the arts. Finally, just behind me was an aging woman working an unrewarding job and looking forward to little. Looking at that woman plodding along just below the hill's crest, I had to wonder what I had really accomplished in those years climbing my hill - what mark I had made on the world.

On the other side, though, lay the greatest surprises of all. On first inspection, I saw the rest of my life as an unmarked slope, a swift slide down to the end. It was what I had been led to expect the second half of life to be. But a closer look revealed tiny figures cavorting through my remaining years on that hillside. Some were gremlins. Some were fairies.

The gremlins were industriously transporting my lost dreams, in chains, from the other side of the hill, hoping to immobilize my heart in grief over their loss. They knew that if they could trap me in regret I would placidly live out my years - never reaching for more, truly being "over-the-hill" in mind and in spirit.

Ah, but the fairies! The fairies were flitting all over the last half of my life, each one with her arms full of late blooming flowers. Each time a fairy would land on a lost dream she would drop a flower and the dream would stir. As I watched, the far side of my hill began to blossom with possibilities.

My eyes opened wide in wonder and, still peeking timidly over the edge at the other side of my hill, I could feel the possibilities drawing me over. I knew that, despite its gentle attractions, I could no longer live my life as I had on my way to the top. If I could entice that creative child of my distant past to join me in stepping over the crest, together we could finally realize our truest potential. We would change the future. With all my lost dreams beginning to stir again, I knew I could bring them to life and with their vitality infusing my heart, I would never be over the hill. Rather, I would hold the high ground, the better to see my limitless future!

> *"We age not because our cells die but because they stop dividing."*
> From "The End of Aging"
> Author unknown
> *Reader's Digest*, November 2003

☙

Ah Spring!

Ah, spring! All around us, the world is bursting with new life. I think spring must be Nature's way of rewarding us for the patience to endure through even the bleakest of times. With the coming of winter, we experience change as a form of dying, but spring's changes are filled with the promise of life.

If we can be so happy to experience the changes of our seasons, can we not also learn to embrace change in our own lives? With the seasons, we know the glorious exuberance of spring will always follow dreary winter. Seeds long buried and hidden from the sun will burst into rainbows of flowers. They are small kernels of optimism that hide within the gloom.

Perhaps the same is also true of other changes in life. I have learned even those changes that at first appear disastrous or distressing eventually lead to some positive outcome. Development of vacant land across the street disrupted my neighborhood for a year, but in time, it brought new neighbors and new friendships. Freeway construction snarled traffic for months, but then gave me easy access to the entire valley. A layoff cost me a job and a generous paycheck, but ultimately left me with the personal freedom I had sought for a lifetime.

Change represents a huge step into the unknown. And so, we avoid it. But in fact, when we accept the changes in our lives, we grow and are renewed. We stay young at heart. Only when we refuse to change do we stagnate and die a slow, premature death. Our thinking becomes narrow and our experience limited. Maybe that comes from resisting the change that is so easily embraced by the young. Perhaps it is how curmudgeons and sourpusses are born.

Far too many of us, on reaching the final half of our lives, grow rigid hearts and inflexible minds. Even though we may have been rebellious or unconventional in our own youth, now the high spirits and marks of individuality that seem to typify children and teens become fodder for complaint and criticism. In truth, they are merely signs of change in a generation seeking its own identity. Were we really any different as we moved from child to adult?

As I grow older, I want to build change into my daily existence. It keeps my perspective fresh, and it's the excitement of handling new experiences that helps me live life with gusto. With change, I can live large because, you see, change is life and to embrace it is to embrace life itself!

"How does one become a butterfly?" she asked pensively. "You must want to fly so much that you are willing to give up being a caterpillar."

Trina Paulus
Hope for the Flowers

☙

The White Suit

It was the best Friday the 13th of my life. And I suppose some might say it was the worst. Box of personal property in hand, I pasted a devastated expression on my face as I walked out the door, but inside, my heart and mind were bouncing like a ping-pong ball. *Whack!* And my heart skipped with joy at finally having the freedom to discover and follow its passion. *Pock, whack!* And my mind rebounded back in shock at losing a job that even though I no longer enjoyed it, still gave me a predictable income.

I have known people who, on losing a long-time job, head for the nearest bar to drown their sorrows. Others slip into tearful depression as they panic over their next step. I did neither. Rather, I celebrated over an all-too-rare lunch out with my favorite cheerleader – my husband Norm. Then I bought a new file cabinet, went home and began the mindless task of catching up on long-overdue filing. Why filing? I have no idea, but I suppose if I am truly honest, I must admit that in its mindlessness, it freed my mind to ponder the next step.

As I filed, I developed what I thought was a good plan for the rest of my professional life. It looked something like: finish the thesis for my MBA, polish my resume, find a job. But my heart quailed at the last step. After all, I had just left a job that with time had become less and less rewarding to my spirit. I was forty-six years old and my heart yearned to break free of all the soul-numbing bonds it had accumulated in a lifetime spent working for others. I wanted professional respect. I wanted creativity. I wanted excitement. I *really* wanted freedom!

Shhhh! I told that inner shout as I gave in to the panic lurking behind all the 'I wants.' *You have to find a job*, I thought. The next week, believing I would soon be on rounds of job interviews, I responded as I often do in times of stress - I went shopping. The result was a very professional new white wool suit to build my confidence. Then I polished that resume, took a deep, resigned breath and began the search. Two self-sabotaged interviews later, with the white suit still hanging in the closet, I knew I had taken the wrong road.

And so, I began peering into my own heart, searching out my deepest passions. As I looked, I began to discover hidden riches. I learned that my motivations were not money and prestige. Creativity and respect, I found, were far greater rewards for my deepest self. With the help of my dearest friends and the support of a generous husband, I began to see faint glimmers of possibility on my horizon. And one day, I began to write.

In a leap of faith, hoping I had a needed talent, I began telling people I was a writer. I printed business cards. I designed a letterhead and a brochure. And I gradually began to believe I was in the writing business. Networking brought me clients, people who, much to my complete amazement, really did not feel comfortable writing. Because words came so easily to me, I believed anyone could write. My growing client list disproved that belief!

In time, I began writing for the simple joy of crafting the words to reveal my heart's deepest feelings. Eventually I risked letting others read what I had written. It was a bridge that, once crossed, could never be crossed again. Just as I must continue breathing, I had to keep writing and releasing my words, like fragile butterflies, into the world, hoping only that they would alight in the hearts of others.

In veering from the corporate superhighway onto this gentle lane I am following, I have tasted the sweet new fruit of respect for my unique talents. For the first time, my confidence and self-esteem have blossomed. For the first time, work is more play than toil. For the first time, I lose track of the day's hours, sometimes leaving my office long after I should have started preparing dinner. Like an oxygen-starved engine at long last finding the air to fire on all cylinders, passion has exploded within my heart. I have discovered the path I was destined to follow.

Not too long ago, I discovered my white suit deep in the recesses of my closet. Its tags still dangled from the sleeve and there was a dark line of dust along the top of each shoulder. Looking at that suit, I realized it was more than just a suit. It was an anchor to a life I no longer need.

You see, I believe that as humans, we fall victim to our own inertia. We cling to past successes and model today and tomorrow to mirror them. In the process, we overlook the potential of the path that beckons us to explore and discover something new. Or, worse yet, we live in fear of repeating past failures and so paralyze our spirits. In either case, we are doomed to repeat the past. It is only in letting go of the past that we can soar, confident and exuberant, into a future of limitless possibility.

And so, I have gently folded that lovely, unworn white suit and passed it on to a shelter for abused women. It no longer serves the woman I have become. But perhaps it will help another let go of where she is and where she has been so she can build her wings and fly with me.

"Be not afraid of growing slowly, be afraid only of standing still."
                                       Chinese Proverb

ಌ

Things Change

I took a different route home from a meeting today. It took me through the neighborhood where I spent my teen years. The neighborhood grocery is a copy center now, the drugstore a rent-a-center. Somehow, I was half expecting to see the same old places. Then I realized – things change.

Puppies become dogs. Children someday become elders. And the things we remember are never the same. The house where we grew up is always smaller, our parents never as tall as we recall. The small town that was so friendly and close when we were children has managed to become a big city filled with the distance of all big cities. Things change.

Some things, when they change, look new and shiny. Others look shabby. That's just how life is. I think we spend a lot of valuable time trying to keep things from changing toward the shabby, frantically searching for anything that will keep our world on the new, shiny side of change. We tear down old buildings because they have become dilapidated. Cosmetics companies are eternally promoting the latest, the newest, the most magical creams and potions to mend our aging faces, bodies, and hair. Meanwhile, plastic surgeons build entire careers on reversing that same aging process. But things change anyway.

It's true. Things do change. I know I have changed. I am no longer the wide-eyed little girl who dreamed she would grow up to design glamorous, sophisticated dresses for the rich and famous. Nor am I the serious student who believed she would follow in her sister's footsteps programming computers or possibly become a world-famous archaeologist. I have moved beyond the young wife dedicated to doing and having it all so she would have the perfect home, the perfect children, the perfect husband, the perfect life. Those were all dreams and, as many dreams are, somewhat unrealistic, perhaps even completely unrealistic. They were wonderful dreams while they were the focus of my life, but things change.

That's OK, though. The wonder and the beauty of it is that I have learned to embrace change however it comes to me. That is not always easy. Sometimes change brings joy, sometimes sadness. But it always brings growth. And so, I have grown into a woman who has learned innumerable lessons along the way. Change was the teacher. I know life has so much more in store for me, both joy and sadness, but I have become a woman who sees the future as filled with excitement. I know that whatever life hands me today will be different tomorrow because, you see, things change.

"There was a disturbance in my heart, a voice that spoke there and said, I want, I want, I want! It happened every afternoon and when I tried to suppress it, it got even stronger."

Saul Bellow

ଓ

Paths to the Future

It's almost June now. School has just ended for the summer. Last night, hearing the familiar strains of Pomp and Circumstance coming across the night air from the high school down the street, I found myself thinking about all the new graduates eagerly anticipating the rest of their lives, excitement shining in their eyes. Paths to the future are clear for some. For others, they are shrouded in mists of uncertainty.

As teenagers, our dreams are large, our expectations of what we will "do" with our lives not yet touched by the stark realities of life. But we learn quickly. At eighteen, I knew I would be a college graduate in four years. But I wasn't. I could clearly see a path before me that led to interesting work and financial success. It didn't. If someone had told me then that at fifty-eight I would be putting my heart on paper for the world to see, I would have laughed and called them crazy. But here I am.

Cathy Marley

I think finding our purpose in life is a little bit like finding our way through one of those mazes students of psychology use to study behavior. Sometimes there are dead ends and we are forced to turn around and begin again. Rarely do we find our way to the cheese without at least a few side trips and fruitless explorations of one path or another. Sometimes we are on the right path but fail to recognize where we are. Usually it takes a lifetime to find our way.

I think my friend Marie discovered her way by listening to the quiet voice of her heart at every turn. When I first met her, she was a single mother working a "job" as a file clerk. Even then, her sparkle was infectious, her depths of character intriguing. Locked within my own expectations of security, I was amazed when she chose to leave that large, secure company with all its benefits and begin waiting tables at our favorite "company" bar just down the street. At the time, I couldn't see that it was her first step on a path to a greater ministry and her own destiny. I suspect she didn't see it either. Now, I can see it was the move she had to make.

Her mind restless, she began taking classes ... first at the local community college, later at the university. Many, many years later, her graduation was an event we all celebrated with her. It was the realization of a goal she could never quite explain, a degree she didn't really "need." You see by the time she wore her maroon cap and gown, she had already achieved what many would consider to be great success. Over the years, she had gone from file clerk in that large, anonymous company to what many considered a step down to waiting tables and then, through sheer tenacity, she found a way to buy the bar where she had started as a waitress. And it had become far more than a bar. It was a welcoming oasis filled with life and Marie's own personality.

Somewhere along the way, though, that education had exposed her to the philosophy of the world's religions. Intrigued, like a fairytale Gretel following a trail of crumbs, she followed where the interest led her, one learning experience after another. Eventually, she found herself, to her own surprise, an ordained minister. Today, the bar is long gone, sold to people more suited to that life. Instead, she ministers in her own way as The Coffee Lady, dispensing fine coffee along with a positive touch to the heart of every visitor to her light, airy shop. It is her way of bringing peace into an unquiet world one mind at a time. Who could have known that would be her truest joy? Certainly not Marie.

When we first set out to conquer the world, we rarely recognize that we must first conquer our own heart. We see life as challenge after challenge, all coming from outside ourselves. But finding our true destiny is more a matter of listening, of hearing, the small still voice inside that says, *This is right*. Although the paths our lives take may be twisted and wander through forests of the soul, they ultimately take us where we belong. I believe they lead us, step by step, into the sunlight of our own truth. That is where we are meant to be.

"Memory is a child walking along the seashore. You never can tell what small pebble it will pick up and store away among its treasured things."
Pierce Harris

☙

Pea Salad

  It's Christmas Eve once again. This morning, as I was cooking for the happy crowd of family soon to arrive, the bittersweet words of *Have Yourself a Merry Little Christmas* stirred sweet memories of my own childhood and the traditions, old and new, that lie at the heart of this treasured family of mine. Hearing *through the years we all will be together*, I realized the only echo of my mother that remains in our traditions is her pea salad. In looking at the rituals our family carries from Christmas to Christmas, I always come back to it. The small ritual of preparing it every Holiday is my way of building a bridge of love from my past to my today and on to my tomorrows.

  I don't know where or when my mother learned to make pea salad. I just know she did - every Thanksgiving and every Christmas. I sometimes imagine her as a young bride, searching through her beloved *Family Circle* and *Woman's Day* magazines for a way to make something festive as she prepared a first holiday meal for her new husband. The recipe box I inherited when she died tells me she learned to be a creative cook by preparing the recipes she found in their pages. Perhaps that is where she learned to make pea salad. I like to think so.

It is a simple dish, but for me its festive blend of crimson pimentos, dark green sweet pickles, creamy golden cheddar and petite peas means Holiday more than all the foods that make up our traditional Holiday meals. For as long as my mother was with us, pea salad was a part of every festive dinner. When she died a young death, my sister and I took up the challenge and learned to make it ourselves. It was one way we could keep her spirit alive and present in our lives.

Reminiscent of that young bride, I introduced my mother's pea salad to my new family the Thanksgiving after I married at twenty-seven. It was my only contribution to the feast my gracious mother-in-law prepared that year. It was received with mixed emotion. Some, my brother-in-law Steven especially, fell in love with it at first bite. Others dislike it to this day. But I have been persistent. Every Christmas and every Thanksgiving, I try just one more time to convert them. Over the years, I've managed to succeed with some. The others, I suppose, are beyond hope. But I will keep trying to convert them anyway.

After thirty-two years, that pea salad, like our Christmas Eve family gatherings, has become a part of our family's tradition. Most take at least a bite. And whether they like it or not, everyone expects to see it on the table. They miss it if it is not there. I suppose I'll be making it for the rest of my life. After all, it is tradition.

Peeking Over the Edge

Over the years, some of our traditions have given way to practical replacements. Others, like the pea salad, endure. As our children and grandchildren have built families of their own, the Christmas morning gift-opening ritual has shifted to a large Christmas Eve gathering – usually at our house - of the entire clan, complete with food and a gift exchange game that is rollicking fun for everyone. It makes Santa Claus so much easier for each family with small children and gives some of us a quiet day to recover from our Holiday preparations. And, while this Christmas Eve gathering is a somewhat new tradition in my own life, it is a tradition solidly anchored in history for our children and grandchildren. For them, that gathering is as much Christmas as Santa Claus.

I sometimes wonder who will make my mother's pea salad when I am gone. I'd like to believe it will be my daughter or one of my daughters-in-law or perhaps even one of my six great-granddaughters who will recognize that this is more than just a simple salad. It is a link to the past, mother to daughter and on into the future. It is tradition. It is love.

I expect many of you will now want to know the recipe for my mother's Pea Salad. Just remember, this recipe is not exact. It has been created from loving memory and as we all know, memories are rarely exact. I usually make it for large crowds and expect to send some home for later. That means I start with six cans of peas, three jars of pimentos and a whole jar of pickles. Everything else is adjusted accordingly. When it tastes "right" to you, you have the proportions the way they need to be for you. Rarely are they the same for any two people. That's part of its charm! Enjoy!

Ethlyn Ellis' Pea Salad

2	Cans of petite green peas
1	Large jar diced pimentos
3-4	Large sweet pickles, chopped
½ cup	Longhorn cheese, diced
1 T	Celery seed
3-4 T	Mayonnaise
	Salt to taste

Mix all ingredients together in a large bowl and chill. Before serving, sprinkle with paprika to, as my mother Eth used to say, "make it pretty."

"The bond that links your true family is not one of blood, but of respect and joy in each other's life. Rarely do members of one family grow up under the same roof."
Richard Bach
Illusions

○౩

Gossamer Threads

When I was a child, one of my closest friends was my cousin Betty. Oh, she had her best friends and I had mine, but there was a closeness that came from the common ground of family. Even though we lived on opposite sides of Texas, somehow we found a way to stay connected. We would write letters and visit during the breaks from school, staying first at her house in Lubbock, next at mine in Garland.

Then, when I was twelve, my mother passed away. By my fourteenth birthday, my father had remarried and we were living in Phoenix. The move and my mother's death loosened my ties with family, especially Betty. Our visits with one another gradually dwindled away to none. Still, we stayed in touch by letter until, with adolescence, then her early marriage, and motherhood, we drifted apart. In time, the letters stopped, too.

More than thirty years passed with little contact outside of Christmas cards signed with love, but not much more. Then, something very natural, but still upsetting, happened. Our parents' generation began to age, and then to die - first our grandfather, then a favorite uncle, a grandmother, aunts, finally her mother and my father. Fully unprepared, we became the oldest generation of our respective families. We found ourselves sitting squarely atop the family structure, with only her failing father remaining to tie us to our parents'' generation. Suddenly family seemed very important!

In no time at all, we had reconnected, deciding it was about time for a grand cousins' reunion, including the two of us and my sister. Deciding to spend several days on a friend's Lake Powell houseboat, we were like little girls planning a first sleepover. Telephone calls and emails flew back and forth from Phoenix to Lubbock, to Kailua all the way across the ocean in Hawaii. Then at last the time came. First my sister flew in from Hawaii, then the two of us made the trip to the airport for the cousin we had not seen in what seemed a lifetime.

With hugs and excited girl-chatter, it was as if those thirty years had never happened. There we were, all well beyond fifty, all talking at once and all instantly transported back to a time of giddy joy, a time when my cousin was one of my best friends and her visits were highlights to be savored with breathless anticipation. Somehow transcending our separation, the blood ties remained powerful, the love stronger than ever.

Now, we have vowed to never again be so far apart and to hold high the torch illuminating our children's connection to their past, a past that gently enfolds us all in the gossamer threads of family love! They are the threads that gently stretch from generation to generation, tying our hearts, our very existence to those who came before, our mothers and our grandmothers and their mothers before them, then stretching to enfold the generations yet to come. Like a sensitive web, they are the threads that telegraph our love on and on and on, ever on.

> *"The most important thing she'd learned over the years was that there was no way to be a perfect mother and a million ways to be a good one."*
>
> Jill Churchill,
> *O Magazine*, May 2003

☙

Just a Stepmother

When I first applied for membership in a business organization for entrepreneurial mothers, I wasn't sure I qualified. My thinking was, *I'm not <u>really</u> a mother. I'm only a stepmother.* Boy, did I miss the mark with that thought! "Only a stepmother!" What a load of hooey!

Thinking about the role I took on when I became a stepmother at twenty-seven, I realized it was a choice that set me up to leap hurdles every single day. Some days, the challenges were baby steps, something as small as my right to choose the evening's television fare. Other times, those hurdles felt like the Great Wall of China. I realized that successful stepmothering often takes more work than successful mothering, not less. I think that is because the pains of childbirth give mothers a natural authority that stepmothers must learn.

And then, of course, there is the "evil stepmother" story that every stepmother must somehow overcome. Thanks in large part to fairy tales such as

Cinderella and Snow White, the world expects a stepmother to be cruel and unloving. I suppose it is a reputation some stepmothers have earned. Those of us who choose to mother other women's children must learn to love these child-strangers who come as a part of a marriage we wanted. Some never learn. And we must earn our new family's love, trust, and respect. Some never do.

Having spent my teen years with a stepmother of my own, I know just how difficult stepchildren can be. You see I was the child who angrily tossed my distrust at the heart of a woman who wanted only to help me learn to be a strong individual with skills to take me through life. Now, having walked in her shoes, I see that she was faced with a Herculean task. At thirteen, I had read all the fairy tales and on some level, perhaps not conscious, but there just the same, I believed them. The truth was, she was merely a woman who had fallen in love with a man who brought motherless children into the relationship. She chose to love us too.

I like to believe that I don't fit the fairy-tale image of the evil stepmother. Fortunately, my stepchildren seem to agree with that. Since I know I will never bear babies of my own, I'm incredibly proud to call these three beautiful people "my" children. They have taught me the rewards of motherhood as well as the heartbreak. In my heart, small moments, taken for granted by many mothers, mark my transition over the years from "Dad's new wife" to "Mom." I treasure the memories of my first Mother's Day card, a son choosing to call me Mom (at least part of the time), confidences

Peeking Over the Edge

shared, advice sought, and grandchildren who accept me as just another grandmother.

Perhaps the greatest validation, though, came from their natural mother who freely acknowledged the positive impact I've had on the lives of "our" children and reminded me, when I most needed to hear it, of the respect they hold for me. Sadly, in recent years I have seen her slowly lose many of her mental abilities and slip from the mother role into one much closer to child. I find "our" children turning to me for support as they deal with the gradual fading of their mother. It is a very subtle shifting of the reins of family responsibility from her somewhat older generation to my own intermediate one. And it is a show of respect that I never expected. Even so, I view these changes with mixed emotion. Cherishing the respect, I am still saddened for this generous woman and for the children we love together. My heart aches with the knowledge of the loss I see coming in the not too distant future.

As I solemnly step into my new position within this family of my heart, I pray I can be the mother they need. But I think that may be the prayer uttered by every mother since time began. Perhaps that makes me a mom after all!

"Life is not a journey to the grave with the intention of arriving safely in a pretty and well preserved body, but rather to skid in broadside, thoroughly used up, totally worn out, and loudly proclaiming -- "WOW-- What a Ride!"*

Author unknown

☙

Esther's Shoes

I remember Esther's shoes most of all. Often a fashion plate, she wore the most impractical of shoes, even well into her eighties. Little-old-lady tennie runners were not for this woman! They made her feet, as she emphatically told us all, far too hot. Instead, there were sandals of every description and color – always with a small heel or wedge to accommodate a poorly-healed leg fracture that, though it left her with one heel permanently raised, never slowed her down. She wore her shoes forever, often far beyond the point of shabby. Those she loved, like her family, were never rejected. And like people who took advantage of her good nature once too often, shoes that chafed or bound were soon out of her life.

From the day I knew I would marry her son until the day she died, Esther was a ***presence*** in our world, the center of our family. She was advisor, cheerleader, financial consultant, touchstone to each of her four sons and the three generations that followed them. A wrong done to any of us would bring her rushing to the fray, sparks flying from her eyes like a fierce mother bear protecting her cubs. She showed me what it meant to be a mother.

This was a woman who lived every moment of her life. In an era when a woman's pre-ordained role was wife and mother and little more, she buried two husbands and divorced another. At the same time, she raised four sons, worked in a succession of offices and eventually ran a business. Esther's self-reliance made her a woman ahead of her time, just a little bit of a feminist far before feminism had a name. She taught me the power of hard-earned independence.

Financially secure in her later years, she had the freedom to do as she pleased. She chose to live every moment, often entertaining the youngest members of the family, the babies and children she adored, with trips to the beach and Legoland, Ice Capades and circuses, toys and games, all flavored by her undying zest for life. For her grandchildren, she cheered in bleachers, applauded at recitals, danced at weddings, showered gifts upon mothers-to-be. She showed me how to keep my heart young.

Irate at being denied sufficient jet ski time on a family houseboat outing to Lake Powell, she insisted on buying her own ski, a brand new powerful Kawasaki 1100. That sleek red and black machine flew across the water. In her sporty red life vest, Esther, her hand on the throttle, beaming smile resolutely in place, never looked back. She taught me to cherish excitement as long as I live.

Peeking Over the Edge

Summers were spent near her beloved ocean, reveling in the salty tang of the cool sea air. Every day at low tide, neighbors would smile and wave as this indomitable eighty-nine-year old woman with the incandescent smile trekked 125 steps down the cliff, boogie board in hand, to ride the waves. She showed us all how to live.

And in living to the very margins of existence she showed us how to die. It was a death made more bittersweet by one last day spent saturating every moment with what she loved most in life - swimming in the ocean, breathing the sunny, fresh southern California air, holding the sight of a treasured son and grandchildren close to her heart. That day, one week before her ninetieth birthday, she stepped from the ocean and as she waved, smiling to her loved ones, her spirit wrapped itself around the memory and flew away. Oh yes, she showed us how to die.

Some women's shoes are so very much harder to fill than others. It has nothing to do with the size of their foot. It has everything to do with the size of their heart. Esther was one of those women. When she left, she passed her matriarchal role to three of us –Susanne, Susan and me, daughters-in-law all. We are still trying to fill her shoes.

"Now is the only time there is. Make your now wow, your minutes miracles, and your days pay. Your life will have been magnificently lived and invested, and when you die you will have made a difference."
                               Mark Victor Hansen

Remember Me

In recent months, wherever I turn, I seem to come face to face with life's transience. Over two hundred souls board a plane bound for business, pleasure, or duty. Fate steps in and in an instant, families are left to grieve. A single cell mutates and a cherished family member begins a long battle for life. An elderly friend settles in for a good night's rest and gently drifts away. Fate walks among us and, seemingly on a whim, selects. Surely for most, that selection comes as a surprise.

I hope my own end will be far in the future, but I expect when it does come, it will likely still be a surprise. I find myself asking, *if tomorrow were my last day, what would be my legacy? Have I touched others as I've passed through this life?* I know I want to be remembered, but how?

When I am gone, I want to be remembered for the kindness I've shown, the goodness I've done. I want others to recall the size of my heart - not that of my bank account. In all my dealings with others, I choose to observe the southern tradition of *lagniappe* - giving something extra by way of good measure. I want to be remembered, always, for going that extra distance. I can only hope my legacy will be one of generosity, love and kindness.

I've heard it said the sincerest form of flattery is imitation. If so, then does it not also follow the truest form of remembrance for a life well lived is to follow that person's example by adopting their best qualities? My dream is that, when I am gone, those I leave behind will be a little more generous, a lot kinder, and far more loving for having known me. What greater tribute could anyone ask?

> *"Strange, isn't it? Each man's life touches so many other lives, and when he isn't around, he leaves an awful hole, doesn't he?"*
>
> Henry Travers talking to James Stewart in *It's a Wonderful Life*

☙

Ripples in a Pond

We called it Dream Builders. There were three of us and we were the very best of friends, knowing each other from the heart out. We came together in mutual need, each ready to re-create some critical part of our own life. Elaine, ever practical and solidly grounded, had a clear vision of herself away from the corporate life and in a business that would impact the lives of children. Anita, our altruist, dreamed of stirring women's hearts, of inspiring them to discover their own greatness. And me? All I wanted was to find my truest life's work, some long-forgotten passion that could replace the stagnant "job" I had just lost to a reduction in force.

We met once a week and, very much on purpose, held each other accountable for taking the small steps we needed to reach our goals. At each meeting's end, we would have defined the next step – our homework for the week. As time went on, we discovered our paths were becoming ever clearer, the goals more attainable.

Cathy Marley

When we finally ended our sessions months later, we had all realized a dream with the help of our truest friends. Elaine was opening her very first business, a franchise where she taught computer skills to children. Anita's newsletter, *Women in Transition*, was an inspired work filled with articles for creating a balanced life. And me? I had started to write. First press releases, letters and articles for businesses – it satisfied that need for a career - then pieces for my own soul.

What we didn't, couldn't, know at the time was that we were creating ripples in the pond of life. Oh, but as time went on, we learned.

Our Elainie spent countless hours patiently teaching small children the mysteries of the computer. The children who passed through her center quickly owned the skills that would take them successfully through years of school in a brave new world of technology that was open to even the smallest child. One particularly bright, inquisitive young girl, a budding entrepreneur of eleven, created her own business, complete with a business plan and business cards, then with a simple press release, became an inspirational story for children of all ages in the local newspaper. Her future was changed in the course of one class. Who knows what path of leadership her life will take? She was but one ripple in Elaine's pond.

Anita's baby, *Women in Transition*, we freely distributed, with love, to any and all comers, only trusting that it would reach the hearts that needed it. Oh, and it did find its target! We have seen the ripples it created, but we may never see all the shores it has touched. In its pages, one woman, my husband's assistant, found the courage to change the course of her life. At an age when many women look forward only to retirement, she chose to quit her job, return to school, and begin working with recovering addicts and AIDS patients.

Years later as I attended Denise's memorial service after her death, I was reminded again that none of us ever knows how far the ripples will reach when we drop our pebble in the pond, what distant shores may be changed by their gentle wash. One after another, I heard of the lives this one woman had saved. In the few years she had worked with these lost souls, she had saved many, leaving them productive and peaceful for the first time in their lives. That day I could see the ripples reaching from our dream of a simple newsletter to this extraordinary woman, then to the lives she changed, and finally to the children they now raise with love rather than neglect. Ours was but a simple dream, yet it touched souls in ever widening circles. Surely that is a legacy worth leaving.

And me? I still write. Only now, I hope to touch more than my own soul. My dream is to touch the hearts and souls of others, to change their perspective in some small positive way, to help reveal the wisdom and the beauty that this life can hold. If I can do that, I can, when the time comes for my last breath, know that I have not left this world untouched, that my spirit will live on. Perhaps my ripples will someday reach shores far beyond my own imagining.

What Is Real?

"What is REAL?" asked the Rabbit one day, when they were lying side by side near the nursery fender, before Nana came to tidy the room. "Does it mean having things that buzz inside you and a stick-out handle?"

"Real isn't how you are made," said the Skin Horse. "It's a thing that happens to you. When a child loves you for a long, long time, not just to play with, but REALLY loves you, then you become Real."

"Does it hurt?" asked the Rabbit.

"Sometimes," said the Skin Horse, for he was always truthful. "When you are Real you don't mind being hurt."

"Does it happen all at once, like being wound up," he asked, "or bit by bit?"

"It doesn't happen all at once," said the Skin Horse. "You become. It takes a long time. That's why it doesn't happen often to people who break easily, or have

Cathy Marley

sharp edges, or who have to be carefully kept. Generally, by the time you are Real, most of your hair has been loved off, and your eyes drop out and you get loose in your joints and very shabby. But these things don't matter at all, because once you are Real you can't be ugly, except to people who don't understand."

From *The Velveteen Rabbit*
By Margery Williams

Eagle's Home

There is a place at Lake Powell where I hope my children will one day strew my ashes to the winds and the waters. If you look on a map of the lake, at the far end of the lovely Escalante arm, you will find a tiny side canyon prosaically named Cow Canyon. It is a rather colorless name for one of the most beautiful and peaceful places on earth. I have spent many idle days there, lying back on our boat and quietly philosophizing with my husband Norm and a variety of friends while we are lulled by the gentle slapping of the water on the keel.

This private little backwater of the lake is only accessible at just the right water levels. I suppose its isolation is what makes it a welcome home to the majestic bald eagles that circle overhead as they search for a fishy meal in the waters around us. When they rest, they perch on the face of a cliff that soars what seems to be thousands of feet toward heaven. It is a place where I feel my own spirit fly. We call it by a far more poetic name - Eagle's Home.

When I took the photograph I have used on the cover of this book, our friend Art Eckstat and his cousin Karen Gorman were with us. The silhouette on the hill in the photograph is hers. Hiking as she is along the top of a shadowed hill, there is a sense of adventure and curiosity about what lies on the other side. At the time it was taken, Karen was in transition, moving on to newer and greater things. Several years later, she passed away, but not before she discovered what joys were hidden on the other side of her hill. I believe the photograph's image conveys every message I hope you, my reader, discover in this book.

Photo by Rita Sherman, Captured Moments

About the Author

Cathy Marley is an award-winning freelance writer/author, entrepreneur, wife, mother, grandmother, and great-grandmother. She lives a contented life in Phoenix, Arizona, with Norm, her soul mate and husband of over forty-four years. Fur babies Jake and Molly the dogs, Sugar the cat, and Joe the cat who thinks he is a dog, make for an exciting household. Cathy and Norm's extended family includes Norm's three (now only two on this side) adult children, seven adult grandchildren, and at last count, 14 great grandchildren.

Having spent the first forty years of her life as an eager reader of other people's words, this former aerospace techie dismissed her creative talents for most of her professional life until she discovered her own voice in midlife. She was first published in ***Love in Bloom***, a creative collection of essays, short stories, and poetry from Women Writers of the Desert.

Peeking Over the Edge...views from life's middle, a collection of her own reflections on life as she reached middle-age, followed shortly thereafter. Written for other baby boomers who are "not-so-far-over-the-hill", ***Peeking Over the Edge*** looks at mid-life as the beginning of life's best half. It is one woman's view of the regrets and triumphs of the past balanced by eager anticipation of a future built on wisdom gained along the way.

As a member of Women Writers of the Desert, Cathy formed an enduring friendship with fellow writers Joy Collins and Betts McCalla. That friendship deepened after both Betts and Joy suffered the loss of their husbands and soul mates. As their friend, Cathy sought ways to help them work through their grief and find peace. Her second book, ***Breathing Again – thoughts on life after loss***, arose from that time. It was written from the perspective of someone who wants to understand what a grieving friend is experiencing, and in the truest spirit of friendship, provide love and support as that friend finds his or her way to peace.

Asked what inspires her to write, Cathy says, "I spent a lifetime learning how to love myself. When I turned fifty, it was as if my whole life's experience came together for me and I saw everything filtered through a more positive light than ever before. Now, it's as if the ideas that have been growing in me for years have finally ripened to the point where I have to give them life. It's a transformation that reaches to my core and demands to be shared."

You can contact Cathy Marley at:
Cathy@CathyMarley.com
or through her website:
www.CathyMarley.com

www.ingramcontent.com/pod-product-compliance
Lightning Source LLC
Chambersburg PA
CBHW070736020526
44118CB00035B/1368